YOUR FONDEST DREAM

HOW TO MASTER THE POWER OF CREATIVITY

JIM LEONARD

Author of

Vivation — The Science of Enjoying All of Your Life

VIVATION PUBLISHING CO.

By the same author: Vivation the Science of Enjoying All of Your
Life   ISBN: 0-9610132-0-6 or 0-9610132-4-9

Cover art Copyright © 1989 by Robert Ray Baker, reprinted with
permission.

AUTHOR PHOTO by Clay Miller Studio, Atlanta, GA

Original Pencil Drawings at the start of each part and chapter
Copyright © 1989 by Lloyd Nick, reprinted by permission.

"Vivation" is a service mark of Jim Leonard, Phil Laut, Jeanne Miller,
and Anne Leonard, doing business as Associated Vivation Professionals.
Only currently licensed members of Associated Vivation Professionals
may use the word Vivation in advertising.

First Printing   October 1989

Vivation Publishing Co.
PO Box 8269
Cincinnati, OH 45208 USA
513-321-4405

DEDICATION

To my dear friends and colleagues,
Phil and Jeanne, Julie, and Anne,
who are four of the most creative people I have ever known.

ACKNOWLEDGMENTS

Julie Leonard for editorial assistance.

Anne Jill Leonard for all of her myriad varieties of assistance during the first stages of my writing of this book.

Phil Laut at Vivation Publishing Company for editorial help, publishing expertise, and great ideas over a period of many years of friendship.

My mother, Anna Lee Leonard, who has helped me in so many ways that I can list here only a fraction: inspiration, love, friendship, and being a fine example of the enjoyment of creativity.

David Hines at Celestial Arts Publishing for advice about publishing.

Cynthia Branigan and Daniel Stern for editorial suggestions.

Vangelis whose music has provided an inspiring atmosphere for me during the writing of two books now.

Arnold Patent for the seed idea for the Purpose Process.

Tim Torian for technical expertise about computers.

Rocky Stump for technical expertise about computers and for selling me computer hardware and software better and cheaper than anyone else.

Victor Boc for technical expertise about computers and for helpful editorial suggestions.

Charlie Smith for thinking of the term "Discovery Writing" and for being an endless source of excellent, creative ideas.

The graduates of the Vivation Professional Training at Lake Lanier for bearing with me while I worked on finishing this book.

INTRODUCTION
by Phil Laut

You are already far more naturally creative than you think. Even if you are among the most creative people there are, there is an infinite creative power within you. Even if you consider yourself one of the least creative people that you know, this book can show you how to harness the unused potential of your own personal creativity. Albert Einstein told us, "Imagination matters far more than intelligence." Welcome to the exciting advanture of learning to use your imagination for the benefit, delight, service and profit of everyone.

Your creativity is unique. There is no one else like you. You'll discover that once you start using the practical techniques in this book that you will start expressing your personal values in ways that please you. This is much more fun and much more satisfying than struggling to live up to the norms of others.

Effective use of the principles in this book will not necessarily put an end to hard work. In fact, their use may inspire you to work more. You can be certain that you'll get far more satisfaction and accomplishment from the work that you do. If you are worried about becoming a workaholic, then you can use the methods that Jim describes to come up with creative ways to enjoy your free time.

Anyone who reads a newspaper knows that the world is sorely in need of creative solutions to the social, environmental, political, financial and health problems that confront us today. I was delighted when Jim asked me to publish this, his second, book. I hope you are too.

GUARANTEE

Satisfied customers are the most valued asset of any thriving business. If *Your Fondest Dream* benefits you, please tell your friends and associates about it. If you are not satisfied with this book for any reason, you can receive a full refund from the publisher by returning it to Vivation Publishing Co. within one year of purchase with your sales slip or canceled check.

People whose aid and support make this book possible:

Cover Design: Handy Print, Cincinnati, OH
Typesetting: Reporter Typographics, Cincinnati, OH
Printing: Delta Lithograph, Valencia, CA
Order Fulfillment: The Creative Source, El Toro, CA

TABLE OF CONTENTS

©1989 BY JIM LEONARD

PART I

THE CREATIVE GENIUS WITHIN YOU

CHAPTER 1

YOURS NOW IS THE POWER OF CREATIVITY

Why should you care about becoming more creative? Because developing your creativity is the key to becoming happier, more effective, more fulfilled. Because you want to become even better at what you do. Because, you want to live the best life possible.

The solution to every problem lies in creativity. Beyond that, creativity is the most important ingredient in success with any endeavor. Creativity is even more important to success than persistence, for without creativity a person can persist a very long time at what does not work. No matter what your vocation or avocation, expanding your creativity is the key to improved performance and greater fulfillment.

We humans simply cannot be fulfilled without expressing our highest values in the world. To live life purposefully is what matters most to all of us. To do so requires, above all else, that we be creative.

No matter how creative or uncreative you have believed yourself to be, you can become a lot more creative by following the program presented in this book. You will become happier, healthier, more prosperous and more enthusiastic about life, as a result.

Most people assume that their level of creativity is fixed and unchangeable. They have it in their minds that true creativity is the rare possession of a distant few. No matter how common this myth might be, it is absolutely false.

Consider this: everyone dreams with infinite creativity many times every night. No one dreams uncreatively. There is no gradation of creativity in dreams. Da Vinci, Beethoven and Einstein dreamt exactly as creatively as you do — no more, no less. It therefore must be obvious that everyone has the raw means for creativity equally and infinitely.

Dreaming creatively is not the key to a more productive, fulfilling life, however. The point of this book is for you to get in touch with what you most want in life — "your fondest dream," — and develop the creativity to make that manifest. This is a practical book.

Throughout the entire book I present "processes" (creative activities) for you to use for expanding your creativity in various ways. I did not write this book merely to entertain you for a time and then have you go on with your life the way you did before. I wrote this book to empower you to transform your life by having an experience of creative mastery. I wrote it so that you can be confident of your ability to make all your fondest dreams come true.

My main philosophy is this: Creativity is the natural state of all human beings. The subconscious mind is constantly putting thoughts, ideas, images, etc. into new combinations. Making conscious use of that process is largely a matter of reducing barriers that you erected between the subconscious mind and the conscious mind when you were a child trying to become an adult. In this book I explain step-by-step how to disinhibit your creativity and develop it into a real source of power for the benefit of yourself, your family and the world.

True creativity goes beyond creative thinking into creative action: results matter most of all. Good ideas by themselves are not enough. Creative action always requires of you two additional qualities besides creative thinking: 1. A clear sense of your own values, so that you will know whether what you are creating is what you really want; and 2. Initiative, to make it possible to carry a project through from inception to completion. Developing your creative thinking, discovering what you truly want most and clearing the way to take effective action are all made possible through the methods presented in this book.

Each chapter of this book presents a different set of skills you can develop:

Chapters 2 and 3 tell you how to increase your creativity by cultivating the various personality traits and lifestyle factors that support creativity.

Chapters 4 and 5 present Discovery Writing, the simplest, most effective way to disinhibit your creative flow and apply it to any endeavor.

Reading Chapter 6 and following its instructions will give you a very detailed knowledge of your personal values.

Chapter 7 enables you to discover your purpose in life, i.e., the unique combination of skills and preferences that most enable you to contribute to the world in a fulfilling way.

Chapter 8 tells how to set goals that are truly meaningful to you.

Chapter 9, Creative Time Management, tells step-by-step how to set up an incredibly effective time management system so that you can easily put all your best ideas into action.

Chapter 10, Creative Money Management, shows you how to combine self-help practices with money management in order to see yourself make reliable progress with regards to prosperity. The approach I take to money management is that the number one priority is to spend all your time doing what you love and apply creativity to making that self-supporting and profitable.

Chapters 11-14 present advanced techniques for disinhibiting your creativity by learning to use your emotions to your benefit and by learning to choose consciously the best way of relating to anything for maximizing your ability to use the resources at hand.

The final chapter of the book tells you how to design for yourself your ideal program for increasing your creativity and expressing it meaningfully in the world.

CREATIVITY FOR YOUR WHOLE LIFE

When most people think about creativity they think about things like music, painting, writing, etc. — "the arts." While this book is indeed very useful to people who want to express themselves in the arts, beyond that it is useful to all people who would like to experience improvement, of any nature, in any aspect of their lives. Creativity can be well applied to absolutely every field of human endeavor from the loftiest theoretical physics to the most mundane of day-to-day activities. Money, work, communication, health, emotions, grades in school, and even sexuality all yield to creativity. You can use this book to learn to apply creativity reliably to every aspect of your life.

Life presents myriad problems of every description. The solutions are even more varied than the problems themselves. But the first step in solving any problem is to have a creative breakthrough that gives insight into how to proceed.

As an example, people usually think that money itself is the solution to financial problems. It isn't. This is true because once you have solved the particular problem with money then you no longer have that money for the next problem. Your creativity is available in infinite supply, however. Knowing how to be creative about increasing your income and managing your money is of greater value to you than any amount of money could ever be.

At first you may not expect creativity to solve all your problems for you. After you have experienced creativity solving a few of your problems that had seemed intractable, your expectations will change. By and by it will dawn on you that you don't have to put up with what you don't want. This book will expand your horizons so you can really grasp the scope of what your creativity can do for you.

For those of you who already make your living by being creative, this book will help you to make your work easier and better than ever before.

Since this book is about using your infinite powers of creativity to become happier and more fulfilled, it is necessary that the methods themselves be enjoyable. All of the exercises in this book are more fun than any game. Whether you're already having a lot of fun with your life or not, this book will teach you how to enjoy your life a whole lot more.

WHY AREN'T ADULTS AS CREATIVE AS CHILDREN?

Children are naturally creative. Just pay attention to some seven-year-olds playing together. They have no trouble at all making up creative fantasies, games, etc. Unfortunately, well-meaning but not very creative adults usually manage to educate the creativity out of them. There are several ways that this happens.

Teaching children not to talk about certain things limits their minds very much. It gives them the message that it's not OK even to *think* certain things. As this process of suppressing their self-expression continues they have more and more of the "room" in their minds taken up with self-inhibition. They get to where they cannot think without passing judgment on their own thoughts. In my seminars I have some simple processes that work on this problem very directly and create an immediate improvement in creative self-expression. Although those particular processes are more suitable for seminars than for this book, Chapter 4 enables you to bypass the problem entirely and tap into your own creative flow more easily than you have since your were a child.

Another major inhibitor of creativity is being taught over and over in school to look for the one correct answer. In life there is never a situation where there is one correct answer — there are always infinitely many ways to do anything. In school you have to learn the skill of coming up with the one answer that your teacher was looking for or else you get graded down. The method in Chapter 4 bypasses this problem as well.

Learning by rote memorization is, of course, the least creative thing in the world. Most other forms of learning used in school are better than that but still involve regurgitating other people's thoughts. Even in the rare instance when children are taught to think for themselves, though, they are usually taught only analytical thinking. Analytical thinking is fine and good but it is not creative thinking. Figuring out how something is and why it is that way are useful skills, but not the same as the skill of creating something new. Creative thinking involves *turning off* the analytical, judgmental part of the mind in order to give the subconscious mind a chance to experiment with new things. It is important to give oneself the freedom to think of things in very unconventional ways.

Children also learn from adults to suppress their feelings. Suppressing emotions inhibits creativity both because it builds a bigger barrier between the conscious mind and the subconscious mind and because it leaves the person stuck with negative contexts. Chapter 12 tells how to eliminate suppressed negativity.

I believe that there is a special place in hell reserved for everyone who ever told a child not to daydream! Everyone daydreams and everyone would be better off daydreaming a whole lot more. Anyone who didn't daydream would be incapable of doing anything but the most menial possible work — work better suited to robots and droids than real human beings. Teaching a child to feel guilty about daydreaming is about as sensible as teaching a child to feel guilty about being intelligent or healthy.

A related problem is teaching children to have low expectations for themselves. Guided visualization in which children see themselves accomplishing very great things would make an excellent addition to the weekly curriculum in every school.

All of these problems can be solved by using the methods in this book.

The methods are tried and true. I have taught all of these methods to at least hundreds (and with some of the methods, many thousands) of people in seminars throughout the United States, Canada and Europe.

The methods are simple and they work for everyone. They will work for you if you just follow the instructions and give them a chance. Mostly it will be obvious to you, even before you try them out, that the exercises will work. This is good because it allows you to proceed with self-confidence and enthusiasm. However, please give the exercises a chance even when it's not obvious to you at first that they will work.

THE SKILLS OF HAPPINESS

There are two essential skills of happiness: 1. Being able to enjoy, fully, what you are experiencing now, and 2. Being able to get more of what you want in the future. These two skills are related and both are covered thoroughly in this book.

The initial stages of creativity always involve putting thoughts together in new ways. This is easy to do unless you insist too stubbornly on thinking about things in old ways.

Negativity always locks up the mind up and limits creativity. For example, have you ever watched your behavior when you were in a hurry to get out of the house but you could not find your car keys?

8

If you are like most people, during the acute phase of "frustrated search mode" you will follow a repeating pattern, continuing to look in places where you already looked but did not find them. Frustration is a form of negativity that comes from insisting that something "should" be different from how it is. In an attempt to avoid the uncomfortable feelings associated with not knowing where the keys are, your mind dwells repeatedly on where they "should" be and round and round you go.

The first step in effective problem solving is to make it OK with you that the problem is there to be solved. This involves what I call a change of context, specifically the change of context that I call "integration" because it integrates the situation into your sense of well-being. I doubt that you were taught this skill in grade school, so

New ideas rush into Allen's mind pell-mell, crowding old ones out before they take form or shape.

© 1988 Cowles Syndicate, Inc.

9

the idea of intentionally changing contexts so that a situation stops seeming bad and starts seeming OK may be new to you. Not only that, since this deals with emotions and most people think their emotions are very mysterious, the whole process of integration may even seem a little odd at first. That's OK; I have taught several thousand people how to integrate their emotions and I will teach you how to do it, too. Much of Part III is about how to integrate feelings in order to facilitate clear thinking, creativity, and enthusiastic motivation. In fact Chapter 13 teaches you over 90 different ways to shift anything to a positive context. The skill of integrating is of immense practical value. Not only does it help you feel better emotionally, it allows you to be creative when life most demands creativity of you.

The other skill of happiness, being able to make things better so you get more of what you want, is what creativity is all about.

In order to make things better it is necessary to know what "better" means to you, i.e, it is necessary for you to have a sense of your own values. In this book I use the word "wealth" to mean having what you want according to your own values. Since not everyone wants the same things (and thank God for that!), "wealth" is something different for each person. In order to be purposeful about improving your life you need to know what "wealth" is for you personally.

WHAT IS WEALTH?

My broad definition of "wealth" is matter, energy, thought, or relationships, organized in a way that pleases someone.

As an example of organized matter as a form of wealth, consider a house. When a construction company builds a house they create wealth because organizing the building materials into the form of a house will please someone more than the building materials would have if left in their original form.

As an example of organized energy as a form of wealth, consider electricity. When a utility company operates a hydro-electric dam it converts the energy of falling water into the readily usable energy of electricity, thus creating wealth for many people all at once.

For human beings, thoughts organized so as to please someone are in truth the most important form of wealth. Good ideas create more wealth than any re-organization of matter or energy because good ideas are of infinite value. Any house will eventually revert to a more random form and all the electricity produced by falling water ultimately gets dissipated as heat. But a good idea (forgiveness, for example) continues to create wealth forever. Any time you discover yourself thinking in a way that does not serve you, you can create wealth for yourself instantly by improving the quality of your thoughts. Books, seminars and tapes are all examples of wealth in the form of organized thought.

When I say that relationships organized in ways that please someone are wealth, I am not just talking about happy marriages, supportive friendships and so on. I am also talking about having a career you enjoy, the role in your community you want, the relationship to God that suits you, and, most important, your relationship to yourself.

WHAT IS SERVICE?

Service means the creation of wealth. Another way to say this is that service is reducing randomness. Service is the opposite of entropy. In the absence of consciousness things naturally become more random. If however, you put your consciousness into something, it naturally tends to become better organized along lines that please you. For example, if you give no consciousness to keeping your kitchen neat it will tend to become a mess (you may have noticed). If this process continues long enough (how long is up to you) eventually something about the randomness of the kitchen will probably engage your consciousness again. Then the more you put your consciousness into the kitchen the more it will become organized the way you want it to be, with trash where it belongs, the dishes where they belong, the stains on the dishes where they belong (down the sink), etc. Obviously it is only your opinions about things, i.e., your values, that make the stains down the sink better than the stains being on the dishes.

So you serve a person whenever you organize anything into a form that is more in alignment with that person's values. When you rub my back and I rub yours, the matter and energy in both our backs is better, according to our own personal values, than it was before. Wealth has been created for both of us that was not there before. Some people would probably look at the trade as "I gave something worth $30 and I received something worth $30 so I'm no wealthier, I came out even" but I consider that line of reasoning demented.

You serve yourself, and increase your wealth, whenever you succeed in making anything in your life better according to your own personal values. When you clean your house, play the stereo, read a good book, or work out an issue with your spouse, you have made yourself

11

wealthier. By serving others in ways that don't require you to sacrifice you serve yourself, too.

In general, individuals become wealthier by managing their assets (both spiritual and material) in ways that cause their assets to continue creating more and more wealth. Other people tend to become less wealthy over time because they manage their assets in ways that dissipate them. The same is true of time management. We all have the same amount of time every week. You can manage your time so that you create a lot of wealth for a lot of people or you can manage your time so that you consume wealth and create nothing. The more skillfully you manage what you have, to create wealth for everyone, the more will be given you to manage.

WHAT IS CREATIVITY?

While it is true that "creativity" means different things to different people, I have a very specific definition of what creativity means to me. While I place a very high value on creative thinking, to me creative thinking is only one ingredient in genuine creativity. To me, creativity must involve getting a desirable result.

To me creativity means: On your own initiative organizing matter, energy, thought or relationships in a new way that aligns with your own values better than the older way did.

Because my definition of creativity involves creating something that is desirable to you, you need to have a very clear sense of your own values. You need to know your own values just in order to be certain of what would be an improvement! The Values Process in Chapter 6 will give you, quickly and simply, a more refined sense of your own values than you probably ever even thought about before. It is a process of self-discovery. Your values are to some extent unique to you. I won't try to get you to adopt my values (other than my high value for creativity) because I know that you and I both are better off with you living your life according to your own values and me living my life according to mine. The practical uses of knowing your own values in so much detail are both vast and profound. It will facilitate both your independence and your ability to form alliances that will actually work for you, to name just two.

I will use an example to illustrate the point. Although I want to get people away from thinking of some activities as being inherently creative and others not, I will choose an example of something that everyone acknowledges as being creative: suppose you are an artist and you are painting a picture.

The process starts out with the materials organized in a particular way: the stretched canvas is resting on the easel and the paints of various colors are sealed inside their tubes. You, the artist, must have a sense of your own values even in order to know that you will value a completed painting more than simply leaving the canvas blank and the paints so conveniently organized in their tubes! Furthermore, you need to know what "good art" means to you and to have a sense of what you are trying to do and express in this particular work.

My definition of creativity also requires that you take initiative. In other words you have to be intending to make things better by the actions you are taking.

Suppose you have some canvases and oil paints stored in your basement. Suppose one day you notice a characteristic odor upon entering your basement and you go to your art storage area and find that somehow a large clay bust you carved in college has fallen off its shelf onto your tubes of paint and splattered clay and paint all over a canvas. Even if you think the canvas looks great with its random patterns of clay and paint, you have not done something creative according to my definition because you were not intending to do so. You may have good taste in art to recognize this masterpiece of randomness as being worthwhile but you have not been truly creative, according to me, because you didn't get the result on your own initiative.

Similarly, if you make something at the initiative of someone else that pleases someone else but not you, that is not creativity but thralldom.

For example, suppose you're a short order cook in a restaurant and you make omelet after omelet all day long in a way that pleases the restaurant management but that you just hate. You may be making a living and providing service but you are just not being very creative. If you start your own restaurant and make omelets all day in a way that pleases you, then that truly is creative.

True fulfillment is a result of loving your life and expressing your purpose. It is infinitely expandable. No matter how much you love your life now you can always love your life even more. And no matter how much you have set up your life to express your purpose, you can always find ways to empower your purpose even more.

13

In short, this book can take you from wherever you are now, show you how to become more creative than you ever thought possible and set you well on the road to giving yourself the most fulfilling life you can imagine.

CHAPTER 2

HOW ANYONE CAN BECOME MORE CREATIVE

No matter how creative or uncreative you have been so far in your life, you can become a whole lot more creative, if that is your desire. Undoubtedly you have experienced being more creative some times than others. Did you know though, that you can learn to create those more creative times at will? Did you know that through simple exercises you can make both your most creative times and your least creative times more creative? Did you know that creativity lends itself to increase through exercise even more readily than your muscles do?

You may have some myths about creative people. You may have an image in your mind of "creative types" wearing berets and listening to jazz. Or maybe you imagine the mad inventor working in a basement laboratory. You might even have exaggerated positive images of creative people working together like in the old Dick Van Dyke Show. If you're like most people you certainly think of creative people as being different from yourself, maybe even a little eccentric.

The truth is that there is every kind of creative person. You can be yourself more than ever by increasing your creativity. You will not become more creative by imitating your stereotypes of other creative people.

One of the great myths of creativity is that everything has to be just right in order to be creative. Some people get hung up thinking that their environment has to be perfect first. Many people think they have to be in a "creative mood." Some don't move ahead because they don't feel that they have the support of those around them. It is quite worthwhile to dispel these myths so that you may be in charge of your own creativity.

That your environment has to be right for you to be creative is only true to a limited extent. Obviously being interrupted every thirty seconds is not good for creativity. On the other hand putting off being creative until the environment is just right is not very good for creativity either. Certainly it's good to give yourself everything you want in life including the best environment that you can for being creative. However, you will do better not to think your creativity depends on your environment. I suggest that you learn to think creatively in traffic, at the dentist's office, while waiting for the bus or wherever you find yourself.

Creativity is not a mood and is not dependent on being in any particular mood either. No emotion can stop you from being creative. What can stop you is thinking that the emotion needs to change first before you can start being creative. If emotional well-being were a pre-requisite of creativity most of the great artists, writers, and composers never would have created anything. Besides, you can use creativity to improve your emotional well-being. Part III of this book is largely about learning to manage your mind and your emotions in a way that supports your creativity.

Regarding getting the support of the other people around you, I doubt that any creative person ever has as much of exactly the right kind of support as he or she would like. Like everyone else I'm sure that you would like for the people around you to always say exactly the right things to you and leave you alone to be creative exactly when you want them to, etc. I suggest being grateful for the extent to which people are supportive of you and just getting on with it. Acknowledging the people around you for being as supportive as they are will probably work better for getting more of their support than blaming your lack of creativity on them anyway. Your creativity does not depend on anybody but you.

Some people say that they cannot be creative under pressure. Other people say they can only be creative when they are under pressure. Both types of people are setting themselves up for struggle. On the one hand, when you are under pressure is when you could most benefit from being creative, so if you tell yourself you can't be creative under pressure that's like saying you can't walk when you have some place to go. On the other hand if you think you need pressure to be creative then you will always be creating impending doom in order to kick yourself into creativity.

The truth is that you can learn to be creative whenever and wherever you choose. Acknowledging this truth is an important component of bringing your creativity into continuous use.

QUALITIES TO CULTIVATE TO BECOME MORE CREATIVE

There are certain qualities that support a person in being more creative. These qualities are personality characteristics and lifestyle factors that support one's creativity. These qualities are not something that you possess either 100% or 0%. They are all things that everyone possesses to some extent and that everyone can cultivate more.

My research and work with hundreds of people has shown me that there are twenty of these essential qualities of creativity.

The end of this chapter has a self-evaluation test for determining for yourself just where you stand with regards to these various qualities.

Then Chapter 3 has detailed descriptions of these qualities and tips on cultivating these qualities more.

The point of the self-evaluation test is not to say who can be creative and who can't. You can be (and are) creative even if you are lacking in several of these traits. The point is to describe what is helpful and give you a chance to begin strengthening these qualities in yourself. You might notice that some famous creative people are notoriously weak in some of these traits. It is not necessary to possess all of these traits to be a creative person. However, to the extent that even famous creative people are lacking in one or more of these traits they could be more creative than they are.

If you are deficient enough in any one of these qualities your creativity will suffer. If you identify one or two main deficiencies that have been limiting your creativity, then follow the instructions for improving in that area, you will see a dramatic improvement in the quality of your creativity and your life.

In some cases you may have been in denial about one of these problems limiting you. Perhaps you have been creative in spite of a grave deficiency in one of these areas. No matter what, expanding these qualities in yourself and in your life is a guaranteed method for becoming more creative.

Start with the self-evaluation test. Then read about all the qualities in the next chapter, both the ones you are strong in and the ones you are weak in. You can decide whether and how you will go about strengthening these qualities in yourself.

The qualities I think are most important for being creative are: curiosity, initiative, a flexible mind, high self-esteem, a spirit of lightness, a sure knowledge of your purpose in life, a refined sense of your own values, logic, enthusiasm, diligence, courage, emotional resilience, a service mentality, good health, leisure time, organizational efficiency, effective time management, effective money management, a supportive network of friends, and an effective self-improvement program.

CREATIVITY SELF EXAMINATION

To take this self-evaluation test consider each statement and give yourself a rating from 0 (representing never or to no extent) to 10 (representing always or absolutely). I suggest giving yourself a 0 or a 10 only very rarely, for the most extreme possible situations. Be as honest as possible in your evaluations — don't concern yourself with being positive. It's OK to keep your results absolutely private. It's best if you take a piece of paper and write down your evaluations as you go. However, if you're riding on the subway right now or for some other reason are lacking a piece of paper, you could take the test anyway.

I won't give you any basis for scoring this test at the end (no "If you got 25 or more on initiative then you really do have initiative" sort of thing). Comparing yourself to others or to a made-up standard is not the point of this test. This is a self-evaluation test. Your scores for the various sections will tell you where you are strongest and weakest. This test is designed to provide food for thought.

A. CURIOSITY

1. I am very interested in what causes people to act the way they do. 2. I keep up with news and current events very closely.
3. It is natural for me to ask a lot of questions. 4. I regard life as a learning experience. 5. I am very interested in the inner workings of the common things around me.

B. INITIATIVE

1. When I want something I take responsibility for giving it to myself. 2. I am a natural leader of people. 3. I am excited by trying new things. 4. I believe it is better to attempt something and fail than never to try at all. 5. I have a large preference for being self-employed.

CALLAHAN
© 1989 John Callahan

C. A FLEXIBLE MIND

1. It is natural for me to see every issue from everyone's point of view. 2. I have an easy time visualizing complex objects or scenes. 3. I like finding out that I have been mistaken about something because it means I'm learning something new. 4. I am comfortable with feelings of confusion and indecisiveness. 5. I often find similarities between seemingly dissimilar things.

D. HIGH SELF-ESTEEM

1. I am comfortable in every kind of social situation. 2. I speak my mind even in a roomful of people who disagree with me. 3. It is more important for people to see me as I am than for people to like me. 4. I believe that I deserve to have the best of everything. 5. When I feel guilty or remorseful I learn what I can and forgive myself quickly.

E. A SPIRIT OF LIGHTNESS

1. I often experience that everything is funny in some way. 2. It is natural for me to experience the good in things that might seem bad. 3. It is easy for me to remain cheerful in the presence of negative people. 4. I believe that we are here to enjoy our lives as much as possible. 5. I don't wish anything bad on anyone but only the best for absolutely everyone.

F. A SURE KNOWLEDGE OF YOUR PURPOSE IN LIFE

1. I am strongly aware of making a unique and needed contribution to the World. 2. If I had a billion dollars I would continue doing basically what I'm doing now. 3. I know exactly what I want to accomplish in my life. 4. Making the large decisions in my life generally comes easily. 5. I have aligned everything in my life to supporting my purpose.

G. A REFINED SENSE OF YOUR OWN VALUES

1. I know what I like and what I want in every aspect of my life. 2. I always know why I do what I do. 3. I experience every aspect of my life improving steadily. 4. I generally make the little decisions in my day-to-day life quite effortlessly. 5. I generally experience all parts of myself cooperating together.

H. LOGIC

1. I am good at math. 2. I enjoy playing logic-oriented games such as chess, backgammon, etc. 3. I easily detect flaws in logical presen-

tations. 4. Learning new skills on the computer comes easily to me. 5. I naturally use logic to deduce solutions to many every-day problems.

I. ENTHUSIASM

1. I have a project I'm working on now that gives me great joy. 2. Working toward a goal gives me at least as much pleasure as actually achieving it. 3. I often become so fascinated by what I'm doing that I lose all sense of time. 4. The work I'm doing is very important to me. 5. My work gives me more energy than it consumes.

J. DILIGENCE

1. I know that I can follow even a very long project through to completion. 2. I manifest excellent attention to detail whenever called upon to do so. 3. I am very hard to distract when I'm working on something that matters to me. 4. I have a definite pattern of succeeding at projects that I undertake. 5. Everyone who works with me knows that I can be depended on to do what I say.

K. COURAGE

1. Sometimes the importance of what I'm doing frightens me but I carry on anyway. 2. I do what I think is best regardless of what others might think about it. 3. I take the next step whether or not it feels comfortable. 4. Setbacks and failures merely increase my drive to achieve my goal. 5. I always know that I can depend on myself to do what's best in a crisis.

L. EMOTIONAL RESILIENCE

1. "Bad news" never flusters me for long. 2. I am usually in an upbeat, enthusiastic mood. 3. I have a well-developed skill for causing emotional resolution. 4. I am free from all suppressive bad habits. 5. I almost never take criticism personally.

M. A SERVICE MENTALITY

1. The quality of what I do always matters more to me than the quality of what others do. 2. It is very important to me that I have a positive impact on other people. 3. I am very strongly motivated by a desire to make the world a better place. 4. In any negotiation I always watch out for the other person's interest as much as my own. 5. Contemplating fine points of ethics and morality is fascinating for me.

N. GOOD HEALTH

1. I always feel very well and energetic. 2. I know what my body likes and I am careful to give my body just that. 3. I always sleep well at night and wake up feeling refreshed. 4. My body always stays very near its ideal weight. 5. I frequently participate in vigorous physical activities that I enjoy.

O. LEISURE TIME

1. I give myself an adequate amount of time off by myself every week. 2. I frequently do fun things with my friends and loved ones. 3. My energy feels renewed from week to week. 4. I know what relaxes me and I always include enough relaxing things in my schedule. 5. I am very good at taking vacations that are fun and renewing for me.

P. ORGANIZATIONAL EFFICIENCY

1. In my home and my office I live consistently according to the principle: "A place for everything and everything in its place." 2. It almost never takes me more than 5 minutes to locate anything I possess. 3. I consistently give organization a high enough priority to keep everything organized pretty much all of the time. 4. My work almost never gets back-logged. 5. It is always relatively easy for me to delegate work to others because my organizational systems are so simple and easy to explain.

Q. EFFECTIVE TIME MANAGEMENT

1. I always know I will get all the important things done in a timely way. 2. I always set goals very realistically. 3. I am always on time for appointments. 4. I always plan my projects out very carefully and in detail. 5. I experience being totally in charge of my own time.

R. EFFECTIVE MONEY MANAGEMENT

1. I have savings that increase reliably every month. 2. I always pay all my bills on time. 3. I always feel completely confident and secure about money. 4. I make my money doing what I enjoy. 5. I use my money consciously to make the World a better place.

S. A SUPPORTIVE NETWORK OF FRIENDS

1. I have numerous people whom I call frequently when I need emotional support. 2. My friends are very encouraging when I tell

them about new ideas I am exploring. 3. I have many people in my life whom I relate to on an equal-status peer basis. 4. My friends support me in eliminating bad habits and cultivating good habits. 5. I live in an environment where my friends feel free to come over and be themselves.

T. AN EFFECTIVE SELF-IMPROVEMENT PROGRAM

1. I utilize effective self-help methods of improving myself mentally, physically, spiritually and emotionally. 2. I know exactly what I am presently striving to accomplish with my self-improvement program. 3. I do some self-improvement exercises every day. 4. I frequently enjoy reading self-improvement books, listening to self-improvement tapes and attending self-improvement seminars. 5. I keep my self-improvement program varied and interesting.

The next chapter provides detailed information on how to cultivate each one of these qualities of Creativity.

CHAPTER 3

CULTIVATING THE QUALITIES OF CREATIVITY

Now that you have taken the self-evaluation and assessed which creativity qualities are strongest and which are weakest for you, I will give you some ideas about cultivating the qualities. By "cultivating qualities," I mean intentionally deciding to improve yourself in specific ways and taking effective action to do so. First, I shall make some comments about cultivating qualities in general. Then, with each of the qualities, I shall give a detailed explanation of why and how it is important to creativity and give some ideas on how you can cultivate that quality specifically.

Cultivating qualities is the essence of self-improvement and is a subject that gets far too little attention in our society. Everyone wants to be a better person. Often people have no idea how to go about it. It's amazing to me that cultivating qualities isn't taught in elementary school. It's not even talked about in Church! Here are some very practical ideas for how you can cultivate qualities in yourself effectively:

1. It is very important that you give yourself acknowledgment for possessing the quality as much as you do. This is an essential part of learning to think of yourself as the kind of person who has that quality. Besides that, whatever you focus your mind on tends to increase in your reality (see Chapter 11) so the more you focus on how much you do possess that quality the more it will increase. You aren't infinitely lacking in any of the qualities. Give yourself lots of acknowledgment every time you do something or even think something that is a manifestation of the qualities you are working on. For instance, if you are working on your health, then give yourself much acknowledgment every time you get some exercise or say no to a drink.

2. Spend your time as much as possible with people who are very strong in the qualities that you are weakest in. Because of the Attractive Power of the Mind (chapter 11) you probably have tended to spend your time with people who had very nearly the same strengths and weaknesses as yourself. Very few things influence a person as much as the company they keep. Conscious cultivation of friendships is one of the most powerful of all self-improvement techniques.

3. Use the tools that I teach in the rest of this book. For instance, you can write Discovery Lists of things you could do to increase the quality you're working on. You can use Affirmation Discovery (or any other way of using affirmations) to program your mind with the new ways of thinking. You can use the Integration Methods in Chapter 13 to remove the emotional charge on things that may have driven you to unproductive, compulsive behavior, etc.

4. Once or twice a year retake the self-evaluation to see how you progressed and how things have changed.

Now here's how to cultivate each of the qualities of creativity:

A. CURIOSITY

Curiosity is probably the quality that creative people most share in common. The more you feel a drive to know what underlying forces are at work in the people and things you encounter every day the more creative you will be. Some people seem to be born naturally very curious and want to know everything about everything. These people are usually avid readers — especially of non-fiction. They usually enjoy school, provided (and this is very important) that they are given the leeway to study what interests them. These people like to regard their endeavors as experiments or learning experiences. Naturally they do very well in whatever field they go into because they are the people who become the experts in that field.

Writers are naturally curious about what happens when words get put together in different ways. Artists are curious about how different shapes and colors create different effects. Musicians are fascinated by the ways chord changes can profoundly alter the moods of the listeners. Chemists want to know what happens if you alter molecules in certain ways, etc.

Curiosity can also be described as the willingness to learn and as possessing an open, inquiring mind.

You can cultivate your sense of curiosity by considering what really fascinates you the most and then seeking to learn everything about that. Let the only criterion be what interests you the most. Let yourself study things that your friends would have no idea interested you. Even things your friends wouldn't approve of. When you were a kid maybe you were interested in dinosaurs. Wouldn't you be interested in reading about the vast amount that scientists have learned about dinosaurs since then?

Everybody is interested in something. If you spend months just studying sex, or how to get rich without working, that's fine. Pick a topic and then really cultivate your interest in it. If your interest in it wanes, then start studying whatever you now have enthusiasm for.

Having an inquiring mind is of far greater value than a college education. An open, curious, inquiring mind is like an empty cup that must be filled. By cultivating your own sense of curiosity you will be assured of learning the things that are the most important to you. The ability to educate yourself is of far greater value than any knowledge given you by others, just as it is more valuable to know how to get fish than it is to possess any amount of fish. Those gifted with natural curiosity will usually do better in college and enjoy college more anyway.

Develop a habit of asking questions. Any time you want to know something, boldly ask someone who might know the answer. Even in personal matters, learn to draw information from those around you. If you think you know what someone is getting at in a conversation, but you're not 100% sure, then ask. If you develop this habit you'll be amazed at how much of the time you find out that your assumptions have been wrong and the person was really getting at something else.

Learn to question everything — to take nothing for granted. Question the authorities that provide you with your information. Don't just take what they tell you, especially if it doesn't fully make sense to you. Ask them how they know that what they are saying is true. Seek out reasons to disbelieve everything you hear or read. Look for ways that it doesn't fit in with what you already know (or think you know). Notice your own thoughts and beliefs, and the ones you profess to others, and develop a habit of questioning those as well.

A person with an inquiring mind places a very high value on truth and accuracy. Such a person is always fitting new knowledge into what was known before to see if it fits together in a way that makes sense. If something seems a little bit off then that is valued highly as a stepping stone to new knowledge.

The willingness to find out that you have been wrong is a very important part of having an inquiring mind. A person with a truly inquiring mind will always be glad to find that he or she has been wrong about something because it means learning something valuable now and being more right about it from now on. To have an inquiring mind, cultivate a value for the truth that is greater than the value you place on being right.

The more you are willing to learn from your mistakes the more you will learn and the more willing you will be to endeavor in the first place. Making a mistake is fine if you learn from it. The whole trick is to make sure you learn your lesson the first time. If you are overly negative about making mistakes you won't be open to getting benefit from them and you will then tend to make the same mistakes over and over. There is an English word for this approach to life: "foolishness." Wisdom comes, over the years, by trying a lot of things, making a lot of mistakes and learning from them.

When something isn't working out quite right, don't just look for one cause of the problem. Look for related causes of the problem every place you can think of. For example, if a salesperson's sales are low, look for psychological causes in both the salesperson and the people he or she is trying to sell to. Seek market causes. Look at advertising and product image. Maybe there are demographic or even historical factors. Sometimes you may find a single thread that runs through all of these seemingly disparate approaches, and then you can really get somewhere in finding a solution.

I found some years ago that the best attitude to have about a business project is that it is a learning experience. That the main point is not really to make money or achieve whatever else the goal might seem to be, the main point is to learn as much as possible. This attitude turns even failures into successes. It means that if worst comes to worst you pay money to get an education. I want to point out that people commonly pay money to get an education anyway.

After every project make a list, as long a list as possible, of all the things you learned. Writing it down will do very much to solidify the new learning.

Part of having an inquiring mind is being open to finding solutions and information in new places. Avoid being hasty in deciding where you can learn. If you are strongly political then spend some time reading books by people of the opposite persuasion. Even be open to learning valuable things from people you don't like. If you have to suffer through their company anyway then you might as well find some way to benefit from it.

Another part of having an inquiring mind is the willingness to jot down new ideas that you have and new things that you learn. The most creative people generally carry pocket notebooks or something similar so that they can be creative wherever they find themselves and have convenient access to their best ideas later on. Obviously this quality also depends on having enough self-esteem to think your ideas are worth writing down.

B. INITIATIVE

Since creativity involves doing something in a new way, your relationship to doing things in a new way profoundly affects your creativity. Initiative means taking responsibility for starting something.

Creativity always involves taking initiative. If you are expecting someone else to do everything for you then your creativity will wither.

Creativity is an important part of leadership and leadership is an important part of creativity. Cultivate the willingness to put yourself at risk and try out new ideas.

The opposite of being creative is being stuck in a rut. The advantage of being stuck in a rut is that it is safe. It's familiar, no one can really get to you there. You can reach out and touch the sides. The disadvantage is that the view is not very good.

Creativity involves the willingness to get out of the rut and try something different. If you have a problem or a goal in front of you then obviously everything you've done before that has not produced the result you are after. To get the result you want, you must be willing to try something new.

When people are frustrated and resisting the frustration they typically do the same things over and over again, telling themselves that what they are doing should produce the result they are after. Obviously things are not the way they should be, they are the way they are. If you spend a lot of your time dwelling on how things should be or on how much better things could be if only they were different then I'll bet you tend to block out the feedback the world gives you, too. Creativity requires being in harmony with reality. It is good to be idealistic to some extent but if you want to produce actual results then you will need to be pragmatic enough to dwell on how things really are.

For example, perhaps you were raised to think that happiness should come from fighting your way up the corporate ladder, spending lots of money, and being married and having children. Reality is that some people are happy with that life and some aren't. If you've been unhappy with this lifestyle for ten years, then tell the truth about it and try something else! If you keep on persisting in doing what other people tell you *should* make you happy then life is going to pass you by.

Initiative means being willing to operate without agreement. When you are talking a group into trying something new you will have to operate without agreement at least at the outset. If you feel an emotional need to have everyone's agreement before taking initiative then nothing much new is ever going to come from you. The proof that something works can ordinarily only come after it has been tried out. When you are trying something really innovative you may have to proceed even in the face of scorn and derision until you actually start bringing in the results.

Another aspect of initiative is the willingness to start over. Many people regard having to start over as the worst thing possible. Don't be one of these people. If you have a healthy attitude about starting over you will be a success at everything you ever do because when you have setbacks you will learn quickly and get on with it. If starting over is OK with you then nothing can ever stop you.

C. A FLEXIBLE MIND

To be creative it is essential to have a flexible mind. There is much to this. Basically it means having a wide range of things you can comfortably do with your mind. When you begin practicing yoga you stretch your body in ways that you are not used to. Gradually, movements that were uncomfortable at first become comfortable and then you move on to more difficult postures, deeper stretches, etc. In this way your body gradually become more and more flexible. The same thing applies to your mind. The stretches in your ways of thinking may seem uncomfortable at first but the purpose is to make you more and more comfortable with new ways of thinking.

Unfortunately we are taught almost nothing about having a flexible mind in school. There are always many ways to accomplish anything but we are taught in school to seek the one correct answer. In life there is no such thing as the one correct answer. Expecting there to be one correct answer greatly inhibits creativity. Learn never to stop at one solution, but to continue seeking more solutions even when you have already thought of one. Many times you will thus think of a better solution. In all cases you will increase the flexibility of your mind.

The concept of mental context is important in understanding what having a flexible mind is all about. "Content" means whatever it is that you are contemplating and "context" means the perspective from which you are contemplating it. Truth is a function of context. The truth about anything must be stated extremely differently when the context from which it is considered is changed. For example, is a drop of water a lot of water or a little bit of water? Clearly it is both: from the perspective of the number of molecules of water in a drop it is a huge amount (or from the perspective of a micro-organism); from the perspective of having one drop of water left on your car after you wash it and dry it, it is a very small amount. This principle applies to absolutely everything. Did your mother cook well or poorly for you when you were a child? Clearly this is a matter of context and really has nothing to do with the food itself. Is it easy or hard to make $100,000 a year? Once again, this is just a matter of context.

99% of good mind management is thinking in contexts appropriate to your effectiveness and happiness. Because the mind naturally tends to stay in whatever context it has already been using, changing contexts effectively is really an art. You can learn to change contexts. Part III of this book and essentially all of my first book are about learning to change contexts to maximize your effectiveness and happiness. If you are serious about learning to master your mind there is no substitute for learning these methods.

Always try to see everything from as many different points of view as possible. This will not only make you better at relating to everyone around you but will greatly increase the flexibility of your mind.

It is very important that you know how to suspend judgment so that ideas that initially seem wrong but actually are right can be discovered as such. One of the biggest inhibitors of creativity is passing judgment on ideas too soon. The creative part of your mind and the judgmental part of your mind are very different from one another.

Creativity and spontaneity have a great deal in common. Both are about allowing impulses to arise from the unconscious mind into the conscious mind. Both involve believing that something good might come from something different than what has been done before. The enemy of both creativity and spontaneity is premature judgment. Good judgment is absolutely essential in functioning well in life. And yet if you are too quick to judge new ideas, your creativity will be shut down. To be creative you need to give yourself the space to explore ideas before those ideas are fully formed.

Certainly during the practical phase of a creative project, the phase when you actually bring your idea into manifestation in the World, you need logic, good judgment, discipline and persistence. But it is quite important to realize that the idea-seeking phase and the practical phase are very different from one another. In the phase when you are seeking a creative breakthrough you need to be able to suspend judgment or you will get nowhere.

In the next chapter I shall teach you a simple method of bypassing the premature judgment part of your mind so that you can get new ideas in overflowing abundance.

Part of flexibility is being able to think both logically and illogically. Many people are comfortable only with one or the other. Both these kinds of thinking are equally important to creativity, to accomplishing anything worthwhile in life.

Logic tends to be very rigid. This rigidity can get in the way of creative thinking, especially during the early phases of it. The new ideas may have a different logic than the ideas you've had before, so the new ideas would never come about from the old logic. It is necessary to suspend the old logic to let the new ideas and their new logic emerge.

An example is: People had to let go of what they thought they knew about flight from lighter-than-air craft in order to discover the truths about heavier-than-air flight. Another example is that people had to let go of what they knew about the nature of matter and energy from Newtonian physics in order to be open to understanding Einstein and atomic energy.

Some examples of useful illogical thinking are metaphor, ambiguity and emotion.

Metaphor means substituting one thing for another in your thinking. By doing that you can discover whether some properties of the one are true also for the other. Notice the ways in which apparently dissimilar things are actually similar. For example, notice the ways in which airplanes are like sailboats, notice the ways in which crystals are like cannon balls, the ways that fish are like birds, etc.

We are taught to avoid ambiguity, but in the initial stages of getting a new idea ambiguity can be a great blessing. Ambiguity has a flexibility in it that can be of great use in finding a flexible solution to a problem.

Similarly, disorder is not a bad thing either, because in disorder comes new possibilities for new kinds of order. An example of this is the animals and shapes one sees when looking at puffy clouds. Or the symbolic meaning one can get from looking at ink blots.

Learn to see the possibilities in partial truths. A little bit of knowledge can be very useful. Be sure you can differentiate clearly between what you know, what you think you know, and what you don't know. By holding the information that you know is right in your mind and then varying the parts you don't know, you can achieve creative breakthroughs.

Learn to hold more than one idea at a time. This is not difficult. Notice that you can easily see a glass as both half-empty and half-full simultaneously.

Ask what-if questions. What if sales suddenly doubled? What if the material this object is made of could be soft and flexible? What if the poles melt and the seas rise? What if everyone learned to manage their emotions effectively?

Emotion governs people's thinking and behavior to an extreme degree and is extremely different from logic. If people were really as logical as they like to think they are they would behave very differently. A colossal example is the nuclear arms race. This is built entirely on emotions of hatred and distrust; nothing in all of human history has been as illogical. If you insist too rigidly on being logical you will never understand people at all when they are being emotional. If you are working on anything that will interface with human behavior then you must take emotions into account if you are to have any degree of success. If humankind ever finds a solution to the nuclear arms race the solution is going to deal more with emotions than with logic.

Most people do everything they can to avoid feelings of confusion or indecisiveness. This is not necessary however. If you can accept your feelings of confusion then you can find all sorts of new creative power available to you. Confusion means you are seeing several different ways of looking at something simultaneously. Than means that you are in a place of choice. A very empowering exercise: whenever you feel confused, focus on what the confusion feels like and try to hold onto the confusion for as long as possible. An added benefit — if you become comfortable with confusion it will be very difficult for someone to talk you into something by confusing you.

Another quality for creativity is a proclivity to challenge all rules. Acceptance of rules blindly leads to nothing new. Always ask why. Why must I solve the problem in this way? Why must I have a job if I want to make money? Why is death inevitable?

The willingness to break taboos can be a major asset in cultivating a flexible mind. If you take taboos seriously then they will build a wall around your mind that will keep your from thinking clearly. Taking a taboo seriously creates the illusion that you must be very careful what you allow yourself to think. You'll find yourself going into internal conflict at any approach to the taboo subject. Creativity in many areas of your mind will be shut down by this process. If you want to be creative then you want your mind to be able to think every kind of thought. Start noticing what the people around you instinctively avoid talking about. Taboos vary tremendously from one subculture to another. For some people talking about sex is taboo. For some young men it is almost taboo not to talk about sex, except that it is still taboo to discuss homosexuality. In some subcultures it is taboo to talk about benefits of Communism; in others it is taboo to talk about the benefits of Republicanism. In the early days of the Rebirthing community it was taboo to talk about death. Question your own personal taboos and the ones you were raised with. Jokes about taboo subjects can be a good way out of the taboo box.

A related quality is the willingness to become unattached to your own old ideas. You may have been raised to think that all people of a certain nationality or political affiliation are a certain way. Once you are willing to let this belief be challenged you discover that it isn't that way at all. If you have always believed that glass is clear, you'll never notice important exceptions. People used to assume that they could not fly. Perhaps you thought that since your father was macho, then you have to be macho, too. Maybe you thought you weren't creative, or musical or you couldn't read well. Without a doubt there are many old beliefs that you have that it would serve you to change.

Unlearning is of great value in becoming more creative. It is necessary to unlearn all the things that you have held to be true but that don't serve your purpose. Throughout life, but especially in childhood, everyone learns many things that simply aren't true. If you cling to your beliefs then you will spend a lot of your time being stuck in your thinking. Additionally, if you want to be really creative, you are going to have to unlearn all the ideas you have about how things should be. Only by unlearning the "shoulds" can you come to terms with how things really are.

Cultivate a willingness to dwell on the unusual. This will help you expand the boundaries of what you can think about. Read anthropological accounts of how other cultures have solved the same problems we have but in very different ways. Read science fiction stories. Watch shows like Twilight Zone. Spend time with eccentric people.

Cultivate an ability to think imaginatively. Write some science fiction stories, yourself. Look at common objects and imagine varying just one property of those. Spend some time listening to evocative music and letting your mind trip out into other worlds. Learn to imagine things that seem to be entirely contrary to reality.

Besides letting your imagination run wild, also learn to control your imagination. Learn to make your imagination do your bidding. There are many ways you can do this. It is very good to daydream about spectacular successes for yourself. Bring into this kind of imagining as much detail as possible. Get all of your internal senses involved, including touch, smell and taste. You can daydream about what you could do to win the Nobel Prize. You can imagine the problems that might arise and then imagine solving all the problems.

Especially practice visualizing. Everyone can visualize; some people are just more in practice at it than others. Try exercises like these: Visualize something simple and then visualize it changing color. Imagine the bottom half of it expanding and coming up and encircling the upper part of it. Imagine it dividing in half. Then visualize each of those dividing in half, etc. See how many divisions you can go through and still keep the whole thing visualized.

You may have been taught at an early age by some unimaginative person that it is bad to daydream. Unlearn that! Almost everything good in the modern world started as somebody's daydream.

A flexible mind means an open mind, too. It is good to be skeptical, to not believe in something without direct experience. But there is a world of difference between skepticism and closed-mindedness. Skeptics get more direct experience than do people who believe what they are told without question. But the closed-minded get the least direct experience of all.

D. HIGH SELF-ESTEEM

Your self-esteem means your opinions of yourself, whether you think you are a good person, with worthwhile ideas who deserves to have good things in life or a complete degenerate who deserves to suffer then die and then suffer some more.

You have to have high self-esteem to be creative. You must have enough self-esteem to think that a new idea that you have is worth something. You also need high self-esteem to think that you deserve to get the benefits of your creativity. If you think that you deserve punishment then you are very likely to lock yourself into situations in your life that you don't like.

The opposite of high self-esteem is self-hatred. Sometimes people hate themselves all their lives for things that happened in their childhood. If you want to raise your self-esteem, then self-forgiveness is very important. Self-esteem means having compassion for your own humanness.

High self-esteem means loving yourself unconditionally. It means loving yourself even when you have just committed a social gaffe, lost money in a business venture, or realized that you've wasted most of your adult life. It represents a healthy sense of perspective.

High self-esteem means being a good friend to yourself. Some of the things you probably expect your friends to do for you are: to stick up for you in an argument with someone else, criticize you

OLD DOG/ NEW TRICK

MICK STEVENS

© 1989 Mick Stevens

Reprinted by permission.

gently, praise you for things you do well, make you feel loved, keep agreements with you, forgive you when you make mistakes, be good company for you, and be there for you when you need them. If you do all of these things for yourself then you have high self-esteem.

Another characteristic of self-esteem is willingness to make mistakes and learn from them. In every mistake is the seed of learning. When you are doing new things you are bound to make mistakes some of the time. If you aren't making any mistakes you probably aren't making anything else either.

Another characteristic of self-esteem is willingness to take risks. If you tell yourself all the time that you are stupid and can't do anything right then you will naturally avoid taking any risks. If you lack the self-confidence to take risks then you will always do things in the same old safe way and never try anything new. In that case you will obviously not be very creative, either.

Do you love challenge? You can. Learn to have a healthy desire for challenge. Learn to like flexing your mental and your physical muscles. The point of being tested is to learn. Welcome all kinds of tests in life for the learning you will get from them.

Another characteristic is willingness to be foolish or to look foolish to others. If "looking good" is very important to you then you don't really have very high self-esteem — and you won't be willing to try new things enough to let yourself be very creative.

Contrary to popular belief, high self-esteem is a close relative of humility. A person with high self-esteem doesn't need to have an exaggerated sense of self-importance or of being superior to others. A person with high self-esteem has a healthy attitude about his or her own faults and doesn't feel a need to deny them. With a healthy attitude about one's own faults, humility is a natural consequence.

A person who has high self-esteem feels neither particularly superior nor particularly inferior to others.

One of the best ways to increase your self-esteem is by raising the amount that you value all human beings. If you value humans simply for their humanness then you aren't going to think that you need to be a certain way to deserve your own love and respect either.

Learn to be motivated by your own values. To the extent that you are motivated by other people's values you have self-esteem low enough to think that other people's ways of thinking are superior to your own. In Chapter 6 is a process for discovering your values.

Few people can really accept criticism well. Accepting criticism well means several things: that you really listen to it, that you not take it personally, that you welcome it, that you be open to learning from it, that you always make your self-evaluation more important than the opinions of anyone else and that you take what is useful to you and leave the rest.

Increasing the love and compassion you feel for your parents is a very effective way to increase your self-esteem. If you tell yourself that you weren't raised very well, then you are going to tell yourself that there are things wrong with you that came from that. If you think your parents are bad then you are going to think that the fruit of their loins (you) must be bad also. Also you are inevitably going to find fault with yourself for all the same things that you find fault with anybody for, especially your parents. Your parents are not just folks you try to visit as often as you can at the holidays. You carry your "parents" around inside you all the time as well. If you are not at peace with these internal "parents" then you cannot possibly be at peace with yourself. One of the best ways to make peace with these "parents" is to make peace with your external parents as well. Often people think that their relationship with their parents would be all right if their parents just improved their opinions of them, but really everything in your relationship with your parents will be cleared up if you stop being so judgmental of them.

E. A SPIRIT OF LIGHTNESS

Another important quality to cultivate in becoming more creative is learning to a have a spirit of lightness about everything. The more you are heavy with yourself, the problems in your life, and the people around you the less creative you will tend to be.

Cultivate the habit of seeing the good in everything. Notice the benefits that you have gotten from things that seemed bad initially. When you think about someone you don't like consider what someone who did like that person would like. When something seems like it isn't going right then start figuring out ways that you could turn the unexpected/unwanted changes to your benefit after all.

Cultivate a sense of humor. Tell jokes whenever you have the opportunity. Go to live comedy. Stand-up comics are among the most creative people in the world and you can learn much about putting ideas to together in new ways from watching them.

Another reason a sense of humor is extremely valuable in being creative is because very often new ideas arise from paradox — from a change of mental context that causes a seemingly untrue statement to become obviously true. It may be a very dry explanation of humor, but humor is actually the resolution of a paradox. When you tell a joke you set up a certain line of reasoning in the buildup and then throw in a twist at the punch line that reveals the whole thing as being a paradox. The more you have a sense of humor the more accustomed you will be to paradox and as a natural consequence the more creative you will be as well.

Cultivate a willingness to contemplate the silly. Silliness has its own kind of logic to it and sometimes that can be the logic that can lead to a creative breakthrough. If you habitually screen the silly out of your thinking then you will have very poor access to the more childlike parts of yourself, which are some of the very most creative parts of you.

Learn to be playful with serious problems. Any goal oriented process can be thought of as being a game. If you regard it as being just a game that will free your mind enormously compared to exaggerating the importance of what you are dealing with.

Learn not to hold a grudge. If you hold a grudge then every time you think about something that reminds you of the blamed person you are going to get heavy and negative and want to stop thinking about that. Obviously that will build a wall around your mind that stops your creativity, at least some of the time.

The more you love yourself, others and life itself, the more you will feel inclined to create good things. If you really want to be creative it is important that you cultivate a sense of unconditional love for everyone and everything.

Negative people are almost never creative people. The most negative person in the 20th century had to have been Hitler. Just because he rose to a certain height of power does not mean that he was creative. Remember that the definition of creativity means bringing something about that is good by your own values. I seriously doubt that the absolute devastation of Germany was the result Hitler was after. The most creative people are known for having a generally positive outlook on humanity — Einstein, Disney, Beethoven, etc. Perhaps you can think of a few creative people who have notoriously negative attitudes toward humanity, certain rock musicians perhaps, but just watch what happens as their lives unfold.

F. A SURE KNOWLEDGE OF YOUR PURPOSE IN LIFE

Your purpose in life is your unique contribution you make to the world. You could think of your purpose as being "your mission". You are unique in both your abilities and your values. That uniqueness is what creates your purpose.

Many people go all through their lives and never have a sense of their purpose. This is a terrible shame and is so unnecessary. It is worth doing anything it takes to know your purpose. Fortunately knowing your purpose is quite easy. Chapter 7 describes a very simple process for discovering what your purpose is.

Once you know your purpose in life it is much, much easier to be creative, because you know what to create towards. Trying to be creative in your life when you don't know your purpose is as difficult as trying to prepare dinner when you don't know what is on the menu.

Knowing your purpose supports your self-esteem because it gives you a sense of making a unique and needed contribution to the World.

What's it like to go about life knowing your purpose? It's like knowing for sure that you are motivated by the highest good and that if you had a billion dollars you would continue doing basically what you're doing now.

Knowing your purpose means knowing exactly what you want to accomplish in your life.

Knowing your purpose makes decision making easy, because you simply choose the option that serves your purpose best. When you aren't hassled all the time by struggling with making big decisions it is much easier to be creative.

Knowing your purpose makes everything in your life simpler because knowing your purpose consciously allows you to align everything in your life to your purpose.

G. A REFINED SENSE OF YOUR OWN VALUES

Your values are what you think is worthwhile, desirable and good in life. A value is something that you think is valuable in its own right.

It is impossible to take effective, creative action without knowing your own values. Creativity means putting things together in a new way that is better for you than the older way was. So you have to know what "better" means to you — and that means knowing your own values. If you're writing a mystery novel, for example, you have to know what you, personally, like in mystery novels so you can write it that way. I mainly lead seminars for a living. Before I started leading seminars I took as many of them as I could and I developed a very refined sense of what I like in seminars. Now I lead seminars that, according to what I value in a seminar, are the best in the world.

Your values are what motivate you. All motivation comes from values and anytime you value something you have motivation to increase that in your experience.

It is impossible to emphasize too strongly the importance of having a detailed knowledge of your own values. Without this you will always be run by the values of other people. Additionally you will be plagued by internal conflict.

By "a refined sense of your own values" I mean not just knowing what your values are but also knowing the rank of priorities given to those values. For instance knowing not only that you value both freedom and security but knowing which of those you value more. Knowing whether you value freedom or security more can help enormously with making decisions like whether to be self-employed or have a job or whether to get married or stay single. (I want to point out that most people who either have jobs or are newly self-employed think that there is more security in having a job but most people who have been successfully self-employed for a few years realize that once you know how to make money for yourself that provides more security than any job could.)

Knowing your own values is very important to several aspects of creativity. It is what allows you to know what sorts of endeavors to be creative with. It allows you to know what you think will be an improvement. Without this you could put effort into something that makes your life less happy — as people commonly do. Knowing your own values allows you to understand what motivates you. It will even enhance your understanding of what it is to be a human being — and that is certain to help you with any creative endeavor that is designed to communicate anything to anyone.

Chapter 6 is about developing a refined sense of your own values.

In addition, Chapter 6 tells how to modify your own behavior by changing the priority of your values.

When you know your own values in a detailed way then you can create meaningful goals in your life. If you don't know your own values then there is no point in figuring out any goals because the goals you come up with won't be really your own goals anyhow.

When you know your values in a detailed way then you will always know why you do what you do. Obviously this is very good for your self-esteem. Even if you don't particularly like what you do (which indicates compulsion) knowing why you do it will make it easier for you to have compassion for yourself.

When you know your own values and priorities you will naturally experience every aspect of your life improving steadily. This happens because of the way that knowing and understanding your values reduces your internal conflict and allows all parts of you to cooperate together.

Knowing your own values makes it easy to make choices in your day to day life, because if you choose generally toward the higher priority values you know that you will be as satisfied as possible.

Your values change as time goes on. Part of what there is to personal growth is a changing of values. If you know how to keep track of your changing values you will stay in touch with yourself inn a very useful way. You will tend not to make decisions based on what you would have chosen in the past but instead on what your values are now. The method of discovering your own values that I present in Chapter 6 is so simple, efficient and fun that you can do it as often as you like and stay closely in touch with how you change over time.

H. LOGIC

There are several reasons why I think logic is essential to creativity. Because creativity always involves a linear process of reorganizing materials, ideas, etc. into a new form, logic is indispensable for figuring out the most efficient way to get to the desired result. Logic is necessary for solving problems that come up along the way. Additionally, because other people are logical to some extent, in many creative endeavors it is necessary to accommodate their desire for a logical presentation.

There are many different kinds of logic, each operating on different principles and each useful in its own way. People too often think of rigid, formalized, deductive logic as the only kind. The logic of abstract painting is not like the logic of debate but it does have its own logic. One could say that emotions are not logical but it would be more accurate (and far more useful) to say that emotions have their own kind of logic that is very different from the logic of the mind. Trying to impose one kind of logic on a situation that requires a very different kind of logic produces, logically enough, undesirable results. Trying to tell someone that they logically should be feeling something different than what they are feeling is futile, foolish and cruel.

Dualistic logic and paradoxical logic are very different and are useful for different things. Dualistic logic is based on the idea that something is either one way or another way based on its very nature. Paradoxical logic is based on the idea that something is one way or the other based on how you look at it.

For example, according to dualistic logic, a person is either wealthy or poor, or at least fits somewhere on the scale from wealthy to poor. According to paradoxical logic, even a billionaire can experience the limits of his wealth ("A billion dollars won't buy what it used to." — Nelson Bunker Hunt) and even a homeless person can experience the wealth that is aliveness itself, the wealth of sunsets, simple pleasures etc. The context in which a happy homeless person is wealthier than an unhappy billionaire is one that is useful and appropriate for thinking certain kinds of things.

Paradoxical logic is greatly underutilized in our society. Dualism is an important source of suffering when it is misapplied. Misapplied dualism can result in comparing one's present moment experience to imaginary standards and thus blocking out the pleasure and resource-fulness that is available in the situation one is actually experiencing.

Paradoxical logic greatly increases one's freedom of thought. It makes it easy to choose a new way of looking at something in order to be more effective at using it. It is extremely valuable in every kind of creative endeavor.

Part III of this book is largely about freeing oneself from misapplications of dualism.

Just because dualistic logic is over-utilized and commonly misapplied doesn't mean that it doesn't have it's place though. All linear processes are inherently dualistic.

What I mean by a linear process is a process that involves doing something to create a change over time. An example is a business project. In a business project you start with a concept, experience, people, resources, etc., and carry out a plan over time to achieve a definite goal.

A business project (or any linear process) is inherently dualistic because you have a definite result in mind that you are trying to create. Some activities will bring you closer to that goal whereas others would actually make you further from it. It is essential to use good dualistic logic to differentiate between plans that are likely to make money and plans that are likely to lose money.

Even so, using creativity well in a business project requires that you be able to utilize paradoxical logic, too. When you are looking at the resources of all kinds that are available at the outset, or for solving any kind of problem, it is important not to be too fixed on what they are or what they do. Be open to finding new uses for familiar resources. Accomplishing anything becomes easier when you make the paradoxical shift from seeing how far you are from the goal to seeing how near you are to the goal.

The self-help method known as "Affirmation Proofs" involve an extreme form of paradoxical logic to make positive changes in one's own way of thinking about something. In Affirmation Proofs you identify a thought that it is useful to hold and then identify contexts in which the statement is true. For example, you may find it useful to think "Obviously I am one of the greatest salespeople ever to walk the Earth." Simply repeating that thought over and over cannot possibly produce the benefits that proving it to yourself can. I don't mean proving it by increasing your sales. The point of the affirmation is to increase your sales. I mean taking the factual reality of your situation as it is and finding ways of looking at it in that make it obvious that your really are, right now, one of the greatest salespeople ever.

Another example of differing kinds of logic is one that comes up in medicine: the difference between specialized medicine and holistic medicine. More medical doctors in the United States practice specialized medicine, which means that if someone has a symptom in one part of the body, treatment is designed pretty much for that condition of that part of the body only. Logical enough and often appropriate. On the other hand, holistic medicine considers the entire body, and even the mind and sometimes the spirit in designing a treatment. This approach is often better. This same difference of approach can be applied to many other situations as well. In economics, for example, it is usually a good idea when considering helping one segment to consider the outcome that will have for the economy as a whole.

You can develop your capacity for logic by playing logic-oriented games. Backgammon is an excellent game for that purpose because it teaches you about probability and how to think quickly. Because each game is relatively short, people don't tend to have as much invested in winning each game, unlike chess, for example. Nonetheless, chess is certainly one of the best games for developing logic. I think playing games is for many people one of the best, most direct and most palatable methods for developing logic. Even if you have steadfastly avoided playing games in the past, I suggest trying this approach if you want to expand your grasp of logic for becoming more creative.

Reading books on debate can be extremely helpful in developing a grasp of formal logic. Many excellent debate books have sections on logical fallacies (the "red herring" and "20 million Frenchmen can't be wrong," for example).

Reading chapters 11-14 of this book will do much to help you learn more about paradoxical logic and how it can be applied directly to solving any kind of problem, including emotional problems.

It's certainly an excellent idea, too, simply to pay closer attention to how different people think about things. Try not to be so insistent on calling people wrong if they have a differing point of view. Explore how they have arrived at their conclusions and you may learn about a whole new system of logic that may be useful to you in some situations.

I. ENTHUSIASM

Enthusiasm is obviously one of the most important characteristics of creative people. Enthusiasm provides the motivation and the energy for creative projects. Coming from a place of enthusiasm a person is more likely to manifest the other qualities that support creativity as well.

Although most people would assume that the enthusiasm is created by the creativity, and this is true to some extent, the converse is even more true. Enthusiasm, like happiness, is a skill. Working on similar projects, and thus given similar opportunities for enthusiasm, not all people are equally enthusiastic. If you have many things working against your enthusiasm then no project will make you enthusiastic.

Everybody has felt enthusiasm, but what is it exactly?

Enthusiasm means being in harmony with ALL of the following: your purpose, your goal, your plan, your present situation, your discipline, your task at hand and yourself.

The term I use for the opposite of enthusiasm is "ennui" (pronounced "on we"). Ennui is the feeling of listless boredom that comes from thinking that what one does is of no importance. It is a close relative of depression. Ennui and depression can come from any of the following: not knowing your purpose in life, having no goals or having goals unrelated to your purpose, lack of adequate planning to achieve goals (i.e., helplessness), or from self-hatred. No one is cured of depression until they are enthusiastically working on a project that supports their purpose in life. Anything else is just more suppression on top of depression.

Enthusiasm always involves doing something; it involves the future. To be enthusiastic one must be "looking forward" to something and there must be a sense of participating in achieving the desired result.

Continuously cultivate a spirit of enthusiasm and you will achieve all your goals much faster.

"Hey, Martha! Guess what!"

© Drawing by Geo. Price; © 1966 The New Yorker Magazine, Inc.

Enthusiasm is by far the best kind of motivation. In the absence of enthusiasm, the impetus to get out of bed in the morning and go to work can only come from one kind of negativity or another — fear of being fired, fear of not being the kind of person your parents would approve of, etc.

It is only possible to be enthusiastic when you are motivated by your own values and your own purpose in life. When you are motivated by conforming to the values of others you will never be enthusiastic, just successfully conformist, at best.

Enthusiasm is really two skills: doing what you feel enthusiastic about and feeling enthusiastic about what you do.

Doing what you are enthusiastic about means telling yourself the truth and giving yourself permission. Ask yourself now, "What am I most enthusiastic about?" If you don't feel very enthusiastic about anything anymore, then ask yourself "When I was growing up what did I feel most enthusiastic about?" These questions will give you a sense of where your path of natural enthusiasm lies.

Enthusiasm is definitely not about following the path of least resistance. If you don't assert yourself, the people and circumstances of your life can push you and pull you far from your path of natural enthusiasm. You must take full responsibility for your own enthusiasm, take hold of life with both hands and shape your circumstances to your will, if you are to make your most fulfilling contribution to the World.

Once you know what you are enthusiastic about, then do whatever it takes to set your life up to do that!

Few commonly held beliefs detract from enthusiasm more than the belief that people must spend gigantic portions of their lives working at jobs they don't like just to survive. Obviously there are many people who love their jobs. It looks to me like more people don't, though. Ask yourself this, "If I had a million dollars would I continue working at my present job?" If you answer no, please consider becoming self-employed at what you would enjoy so much that you'd do it without motivation by money. Motivation by money is a wonderful thing unless it is your primary motivation. It is far easier to make a lot of money doing what fulfills you than doing what you do only for the money.

Most people greatly over-estimate the difficulty of being self-employed and greatly under-estimate the benefits and pleasures of self-employment. The main skill you need to be self-employed is the ability to sell. If you can sell, then you can be successfully self-employed; if you can't sell then you probably can't. Anybody can learn how to sell. It just takes practice. If you want to learn how to sell, find some small item that you really like that sells for $5 to $10, find out where to get them at wholesale, and sell them at retail to people you meet. Carry at least one of them with you all the time and give everyone you talk to a chance to buy one. This simple process will teach you how to sell very effectively.

The second skill I mentioned for being enthusiastic is "being enthusiastic about what you are doing." By this I mean being able to integrate setbacks and negative emotions into your sense of enthusiasm so that you can maintain enthusiasm throughout a long project. A discussion of integrating emotions into enthusiasm runs into advanced self-improvement concepts right away because people's emotional responses are so complex and because the emotional training that virtually everyone received in growing up was so poor. The bad news is that the advanced skills needed for staying enthusiastic are not taught in junior high school. The good news is that they are taught in Part II of this book.

The word "enthusiasm" comes from Greek roots meaning "God within". With enthusiasm the best parts of a person become expressed in the World, the "God within" made manifest for the good of all.

J. DILIGENCE

Diligence means attention to detail, discipline and persistence. It means giving your all to your project. Even with enthusiasm you will never accomplish very much without diligence.

Diligence and enthusiasm go hand-in-hand. Attention to detail comes naturally when you are feeling enthusiastic.

Diligence without enthusiasm is a rather nasty thing, like forcing yourself to focus on something loathsome.

An aid to maintaining diligence is to keep a check-list (or several) of the details you need to be monitoring. You can make one neat checklist and photocopy it so that you can literally check the details off each time you are dealing with that aspect of your project. Non-repetitive tasks can be monitored very effectively with the time-management system described in Part III.

Discipline means knowing what to do next to further your project most effectively and then making sure you do that instead of something else. Some of the time this will probably mean doing what serves

49

your project instead of doing what you feel like doing. Many of the urges that arise from the unconscious mind are for things that don't really maximize your well-being. Maintaining discipline is a recognition of this fact.

The purpose of discipline is to create certainty. At several points you will probably need some discipline to keep your creative projects running smoothly. Commit yourself to doing something effective pertaining to achieving your goal every day. Probably the more effectively you cultivate your enthusiasm, the less you will need discipline. In any case it is best to cultivate enthusiasm about your discipline and be disciplined about cultivating your enthusiasm.

The opposite of discipline is compulsion — having the urges that arise from your unconscious mind run your life. Some people think that freedom means freedom to indulge their urges. These people never know true freedom because they are slaves to their compulsion.

Certainly you will want to have enough discipline to not have vices. If you allow yourself to indulge in vices then inevitably the vices will draw the energy that you could otherwise be putting into being creative.

To get what you want in life you must be flexible about your methods and inflexible about your goals. Persistence means being inflexible about your goals. It means hanging in there when the going gets tough. Sometimes it means eating setbacks for breakfast.

Persistence is the second most important ingredient in success of any kind (the first being creativity itself). Clearly you have to stay with something long enough to get a result from it. If you keep trying and failing long enough then success becomes inevitable, assuming that you are learning at least something each time.

Everyone who has ever succeeded at anything has failed at it many times first. What makes a person a winner? A winner is a loser who kept trying. A loser is a loser who gave up and settled for being a loser forever.

K. COURAGE

Courage means staying on purpose regardless of your emotions. Anything new can be depended on to bring up emotions, especially fear. If you lack courage you will never get very far with anything new at all; you'll just stay in your rut — and your fear — forever. You must be courageous to be creative. Otherwise even your best ideas will never get off the ground because you'll give up before you even start.

The biggest inhibitor of creativity is giving up before beginning, which comes from having an unwholesome relationship to fear. Courage is not the same as fearlessness. Courage means going ahead with what needs to be done even in the face of fear. Fear cannot stop you from doing anything. Thinking that the fear needs to go away first before you can proceed is what can stop you.

You might as well assume that there will be setbacks along the way in your creative projects. Courage is the quality that enables you to carry on to success despite setbacks.

Using the methods described in Part II you can learn to transform your fear into alertness and excitement. You still have to have courage even when you have this skill. Just to face the fear, rather than hide from it, you need courage.

Courage comes from knowing that what is there to be done is more important than feeling comfortable. The truth about courage is that you already have plenty. You already know that you can proceed even when you're feeling afraid. Just use the courage that is already there for you and get on with what needs to be done. If you don't feel courageous then just keep emphasizing to yourself how important it is that you carry on with your project. Think how much better you'll feel about yourself if you just take the next step. Realize that the next five years are going to pass quickly anyway and either you will have made a creative contribution or you won't have. Realize that you will never be happy with yourself as a coward because you weren't born to be a coward.

Like every other quality, courage becomes a habit. When it's a habit, it isn't that you won't need as much courage anymore. It's that you'll have the self-esteem to know immediately that is your destiny to take the next step, and the next step, and to succeed.

L. EMOTIONAL RESILIENCE

Emotional resilience means that you can "bounce back" from setbacks easily. It means that if you get bad news, you don't stay negative about it long but rather quickly relax into your feelings about it, notice that all is not lost, and carry on. It means that if you go through a difficult phase in relationship that you take it in stride and get back to a forgiving and loving space very quickly.

Without emotional resilience it is almost impossible to complete any substantial creative project. There are always going to be unexpected difficulties, distractions, activated emotions, etc. Your ability to process your own emotions well and quickly makes a huge difference.

Once component of emotional resilience is optimism. It is important that you expect things to get better. Without this you'll go through life thinking that every setback might be the big one that puts a final limit on your creative expression. Clearly optimism to the point of losing touch with reality does not support creativity, either. But pessimists generally get stopped far too easily to be very productive or creative.

Most of my career has been devoted to helping people to develop emotional resilience. The self-help technique that I developed called "Vivation" is the skill of causing emotional resolution. My field expanded into teaching people how to develop creativity because I noticed that one of the most consistent results that everyone gets from learning how to Vive is a substantial expansion in creativity. Negativity is the main inhibitor of creativity and Vivation is the most effective way of ridding one's own conscious and unconscious mind of negativity. Chapters 11-13 of this book are about developing the ability to ability to focus one's mind on what is good and useful in one's situation, thus resolving emotions and becoming more creative. Reading those chapters will help you to develop emotional resilience even if you never learn to Vive.

M. A SERVICE MENTALITY

You have to value bringing good into the world to be creative. If you are hostile toward the world beyond a certain point, then cross-current desires for bad things to happen to people will interfere with your creativity.

A service mentality means being more concerned about he quality of service that you provide than you are about the quality of service provided by others. In other words it means placing a strong value on serving others, whether or not they have a strong value on serving others.

The truth about us humans is that we are all 99% alike and 1% different. We all have the same things to deal with in life and the same resources for dealing with them, with only relatively subtle variations on the basic themes. To desire good for yourself and bad for others creates an internal inconsistency that will inhibit your creativity and your effectiveness at everything. For this reason it is extremely valuable to purify your thoughts so that you wish everyone well regardless of your judgments of them.

Without a service mentality work cannot be fun. All fulfillment from work comes from having a sense of making the world a better place.

Motivation to make the World a better place is a very strong source of inspiration and creativity. Regardless of what you do for a living I suggest that you figure out all the ways that the World benefits from what you are doing and dwell on that a lot while doing your work.

Part of having a service mentality is scrupulously setting up your life to create win-win situations. Part of this is that when you are negotiating with someone that you keep focused on their getting what they want as well as your getting what you want. There are enormous benefits to doing business in this way. One is that people will want to do business with you. Another is that negotiations will generally proceed easily and quickly. Yet another is that whenever anyone is empowered everyone is empowered and so you receive benefit from the good deal that your "opponent in the negotiation" got from you.

Ethics is the most practical branch of philosophy. Ethics means the study of the effects that your actions have on other people. I suggest that you give a lot of thought to ethics, play mental games with yourself ("If I were in this situation, would I do this or this?") and discuss ethics with others. The more ethically sure of yourself you are the easier it will be for you to proceed with a creative project.

Depending on the company you keep, some of your friends may be very cynical about your cultivating a service mentality. Don't listen to these friends. If they won't be swayed by your arguments in favor of cultivating a service mentality then find new friends. Only friends who bring out the best in you are genuine friends anyway.

Cultivating a service mentality is the best thing you can do on your own behalf. It just might be the key that unlocks the manifestation of all your fondest dreams.

N. GOOD HEALTH

If you are not in good health then your health may very well be the limiting factor to how creative you can be. Obviously this is true if you are so sick that you are confined to bed. It is true in subtler ways as well. You have to have both physical endurance and a steady calmness if you are going to be creatively productive for long stretches of time. Clear thought requires good health of your brain, your entire nervous system, your endocrine system, your circulatory system, your digestion, etc. Almost everything in your body effects your thinking to some extent. Not only that but worrying about your health can occupy your mind in a way that reduces your creativity as well.

Do what it takes to keep yourself in an excellent state of health. Eat right, exercise regularly, get enough rest, get symptoms checked out by a health professional promptly, and quit smoking and taking drugs.

Investigate holistic health practices and engage enthusiastically in the ones you like the best.

This is not mainly a book about health and I'm not going to put my pet health tips in. There are many excellent books about health and you can investigate these or not as you see fit. You probably already have a pretty good idea of what you could do to improve your health anyway.

Obviously you value creativity or you wouldn't be reading this book. What I mean to do in this section is to point out to you that your health and your creativity are intimately connected. I mean to encourage you to increase your value for good health so that you will increase your motivation to do those things that are good for you.

O. LEISURE TIME

Creative people report very, very commonly that they get their best ideas during leisure moments, while taking a walk, while listening to music, even while asleep. A relaxed mind thinks better than a stressful mind. Workaholics are not usually the most creative people, at least not while they are being workaholic. Leisure time means time when you can do whatever you feel like. If you have a life-style that doesn't give you enough time to do whatever you feel like, then change your life-style. If you have feelings of stress build up from week to week, change your life-style to get more leisure time and more stress reduction. Find out what stress-reduction techniques you like. Exercise, being in nature, Vivation, sensory isolation tanks, going to the movies, sex, whatever works for you. Avoid the trap of using alcohol or drugs for stress-reduction, however, because these substances only create an illusion of reduced stress while actually stressing your body even more.

There are two main types of leisure time that everyone needs: leisure time alone and leisure time with friends and loved ones. Make sure that you get adequate amounts of each of these. Without an adequate amount of time alone you will lose your sense of self and define yourself in terms of the roles you play — something that is obviously bad for creativity. Among many benefits, leisure time with your friends and loved ones is necessary for you to get a sense of shared values with others — something that is essential if others are to be recipients of your creativity to any extent.

Perhaps you have always thought that working more would make you more creative. Unless you habitually work very little then working more is very unlikely to increase your creativity. Try working less. The best results come from working smarter not harder.

Taking vacations and other kinds of time off is a skill you can develop. Plan your time off and stick to your plans. After every vacation figure out as well as you can what you could do next time to have an even better vacation. Make sure that you get some leisure time every day and some additional leisure time every week.

Make sure you don't have stress build up from week to week. If you do that then your mental and physical health are going to stop you. Very often people get sick because that's the only time off they give themselves. This is very unsatisfactory way to get time off, obviously. If you give yourself adequate leisure time your physical and mental health and your creativity will benefit enormously.

P. ORGANIZATIONAL EFFICIENCY

The main point of organizational efficiency is to stay out of your own way while working on a project. If you are messy and disorganized, then you will waste a lot of time and energy looking for lost items, being unable to respond to customers' needs, etc. Enthusiasm can be dissipated very quickly by running around, panicking in frustrated search mode.

Organizational efficiency consists mainly of space utilization, "particle management" and developing and maintaining systems. By "space utilization" I mean having shelves, desks, bulletin boards, etc., organized so that you have a handy place for every possession. By "particle management" I mean keeping things filed, having your message book near the phone, having whatever the tools of your trade are near at hand and well kept, etc. You simply must have systems for keeping track of paper flow, correspondence, etc., if you want to get things done well. It is well worth doing whatever it takes to make this work. Even if you delegate a substantial amount of this kind of work to a secretary (an excellent idea!) you still need to be reasonably good at it yourself or you'll be constantly impeding your own progress.

One of the most common causes of chronic organizational inefficiency is rebelliousness stemming from unpleasant childhood experiences. There are tips for overcoming this kind of negativity in Chapter 12.

It is common (though far from universal) for men to have bigger problems with organizational efficiency than women. Men have gotten myriad disadvantages from the patriarchal, sexist, social system that it is presently on its way out. Thinking that some kinds of work are "women's work" is one of the worst of these disadvantages. Men: depending on women to keep your house neat and your life organized disempowers your life and saps your creativity! You don't need this kind of dependency. If you stop thinking that some kinds of work are "beneath you" you'll be far more effective at getting things done and all your relationships with women will become more satisfying, too.

The first step in improving organizational efficiency, once you've decided to do something about it, is to set aside plenty of time for the sole purpose of getting organized. Even if it seems like spending several days on this project is a lot, it will save you many, many days of looking for lost items in the long run.

Plan your systems first. What are the things you need to do on a regular basis? Where will you actually do these things? How best can you (or your secretary) work with these things within the space available? Write down each step of each project — design routines (on paper!). If you work with other people it is important that you consult them about each phase of this.

Next, set up the physical space to support these newly developed systems. File cabinets, shelves, etc., are excellent investments (but certainly shop around to find the best prices!)

It is almost always better to get the new systems started first, so that current things are organized, and then to handle the disorganization from the past once the present is already flowing better. For example, suppose you have boxes of papers in complete disarray. Don't wait until all of that has been sorted and filed to get started filing your incoming correspondence! Set up your file system first, and use it consistently, and as you are able file the materials from the past.

Keep working until you really do have "a place for everything and everything in its place." If you have never had that before, you'll be amazed at how good it feels and how efficiently you can get things done once you achieve it. Frustration is the enemy of enthusiasm and organizational efficiency is the enemy of frustration!

Q. EFFECTIVE TIME MANAGEMENT

To be effective at anything you need to have an effective method of time-management. You need a system that allows you to look at your day-to-day activities and change your routines. You need a system that allows you to keep track of appointments. You need a system that allows you to plan an entire project and have some sense of when you will be doing each step.

One of the important benefits of a time-management system is that it is the cure for overwhelm. Overwhelm comes about when you think you have more to do than you can do. The cure for overwhelm is planning. When you have it figured out when you are going to do each thing, and you can see that you still have an adequate amount of leisure time, then you won't feel overwhelmed anymore. Most people habitually tell themselves that they can get more done in less time than they actually can. They live continuously biting off more than they can chew. Adequate planning makes it easy to say no to new projects that you don't really have time for.

Chapter 9 of this book is about a very simple, very effective, very inexpensive time management system that I have developed over the last ten years and that you can put to use immediately. Even if you already have a time-management system that you like very well, you will find many useful ideas in that part of this book.

R. EFFECTIVE MONEY MANAGEMENT

"Money without purpose is soon spent," — Phil Laut.

If you are not increasing your savings steadily then you are not managing your money adequately. If you have to struggle each month to make ends meet, then that is very likely to interfere with your creativity. If you make your living doing something that you don't enjoy or something that is off purpose for your life — then that is a money management problem, too.

The best goal to have is to have a way of making money that you are enthusiastic about and that serves your purpose and makes you enough money that you can meet all your expenses and increase your savings every month. If this is not your situation then I suggest focusing on your financial situation with enough creativity for long enough to create this. Prosperity is everybody's birthright.

I do not advocate being materialistic. By materialistic I mean thinking that money and material things are what matter most in life. However, my observation has been that people are materialistic in direct proportion to how much they feel that they are up against survival. The poor people on the street in New Delhi were the most materialistic people I ever met. Some people feel emotionally up against survival when they are millionaires. If you are dissatisfied with the service you provide and the life that you live then you may get caught in the trap of thinking that if you just had more money then everything would be fine. If you get money handled so that you can focus on doing what is genuinely satisfying for you then you will almost certainly not be materialistic.

In Part II of this book are some suggestions for money management coordinated with time management.

When you have a clear sense of purpose and a clear sense of your own values and you have money handled in your life, then you can use money creatively to make the world a better place. This does not necessarily involve donating to charities, although that certainly is one good way. You can do this by putting money into your own projects including profit-making projects. If you are doing more to help the world than anyone else that you know of, then I can't think of any good reason to donate to anyone else (except that you might want to, which is certainly a good reason). I do suggest that you put conscious thought into where your money can do the most good for the World.

I also suggest that you discipline your spending so as not to contribute money to causes that are the opposite of your values. This is one strong argument against buying drugs, unless you feel that organized crime supports your purpose in life. Even if you buy drugs from a friend of yours, it is probable that somewhere up the supply line from your friend is a crime organization that perpetrates every sort of atrocity in order to protect their profits — certainly this is true if there is any importing involved.

Creativity and consciousness are closely linked. Putting consciousness into your financial life will increase your creativity. You can also cultivate your creativity and use it to satisfy all your financial desires as well.

S. A SUPPORTIVE NETWORK OF FRIENDS

The people with whom you associate exert a profound influence upon you. It is important to choose your associates carefully. Good supportive friends can do much to make your life more enjoyable and productive. Most creative projects require working with other people for at least some part of the project. Having a network of supportive friends will make it much easier for you make contact with the people your projects need.

It is important to have friends who support you when you are in the germinal phase of new projects. Sometimes you may want to tell your friends about something that they have never heard of before. If they are open-minded even while still skeptical, they are truly supportive friends. If they tease you or discourage you they are not really friends.

Friends can be very helpful when you are wanting to give up bad habits and develop good habits. You don't need friends who resent you for giving up bad habits that they are still indulging.

Friendship requires a mutuality of support. A one-sided relationship is not a true supportive friendship.

It is important to have friends whose judgment you trust so you can ask their advice on a variety of topics. No one has all the answers to everything all the time. Therefore everyone needs friends whose opinions are valued and trustworthy.

Friendships need cultivating. It is important to create the time to spend doing things with your friends.

Everyone sometimes picks up a friend who is a bad influence or who is unsupportive. I suggest being honest with the person about this. If you express your desires for improvement in your relationship, the person may well make an effort to improve. If the person persists in being a bad influence on you or on being unsupportive even after you have told him or her your honest feelings about it, I suggest breaking off your friendship with that person. Certainly still be cordial, but stop spending time with the person. This is not being cold; you have a right and even a duty to get what you want in your relationships!

If you feel like you have a hard time making new friendships, take heart. This is a problem that lends itself very well to self-improvement processing. The exercises in this book are very broadly applicable and can be applied to this problem with very satisfactory results.

59

T. AN EFFECTIVE SELF-IMPROVEMENT PROGRAM

The reason this is so important is two-fold. For one thing, if you are like any normal human being you have some aspects to your personality and your mental make-up that detract from your well-being. If you develop good self-improvement skills you can correct these problems and no longer be troubled by them. For another thing, your life is changing all the time. Your thoughts and habits need to change in response to this. Self-improvement practices can help you make these changes so you can be consistently effective.

This whole book is really about self-improvement, so there's no point in going into a lot of detail about cultivating this particular quality right here. Chapter 10 has detailed instructions for developing an effective self-improvement program regarding money and prosperity. Chapter 15 tells all about developing self-improvement programs in general.

CHAPTER 4

RELIABLE ACCESS TO THE CREATIVE FLOW

As I pointed out in the last chapter, creativity is a close ally of spontaneity; premature negative judgment is its surest enemy. In this chapter I will show you how to overcome premature negative judgment and get access to your creativity quickly, reliably, and enjoyably.

Creative thinking generally takes one of two forms, either a creative breakthrough or the creative flow. A creative breakthrough comes about when you try out a new way of looking at something and gain an insight from the change of context. The creative flow is what you experience when you disinhibit your mind enough to allow ideas to come forth spontaneously and rapidly, one after another. Solving a problem generally comes from having a creative breakthrough. Composing a song, writing a letter or painting a picture generally require tapping in to the creative flow for extended periods of time. Additionally, having access to the creative flow will give you a reliable source of creative breakthroughs.

Creativity almost never comes from going round and round repeating the same thoughts over and over. In order to gain reliable access to either creative breakthrough or the creative flow it is necessary to know how to "turn off" the part of the mind that is rigid and judgmental. You may have noticed that there is a part of your mind that always know how things "should" be. This part of your mind is continuously passing judgment on all your experiences and ideas, comparing them to its own rigid standards. When confronted with a problem or a project this part of your mind insists that you find the one "right way" to handle it. This part of your mind is useful to you in making evaluations, but it probably gets in the way of your creative thinking. Thinking that there is one "right way" makes creative thinking almost impossible because it leads to rigidity and to premature rejection of useful new ideas.

In this chapter I introduce the technique that I call :"Discovery Writing." I wish to caution you that Discovery Writing is so simple that it may look at first like it couldn't be a very powerful process — its simplicity is actually the key to its power. I have been teaching powerful self-help methods to hundreds of people a year for over ten years and I have never seen anything else as effective as this for aiding people in making improvements to their lives. Creativity is the solution to every problem and the most important ingredient in achieving any goal. This process opens a person to the creative flow with absolute reliability. It can focus your innate creativity on whatever problem or goal you choose.

Another hazard of the process being so simple is that people sometimes ignore the simple instructions that do exist. These instructions have come from years of experimentation and experience. I urge you to study the instructions carefully and follow them exactly.

LEARNING TO USE DISCOVERY WRITING

I have found that people learn the technique best when I present it in three steps.

You will need pen and paper (lined is best) while reading this chapter because it is all written processes.

STREAM OF CONSCIOUSNESS WRITING

The simplest method for accessing creativity without blocking it out with premature negative judgment is called Stream-of-Consciousness Writing. The way to do this is to have plenty of paper and just sit and write out all of your thoughts, exactly as they come to mind, for some arbitrary amount of time like 5 minutes. Write down ideas whether or not they seem like they might be valuable. You don't need to share this with anyone so it is OK if some of the things that come to mind would be shocking or embarrassing if they were shared. Keep your pen moving and write as fast as you can; do your best to keep up with the speed of your thoughts. If your pen stops, make it move, even if you wind up writing out gibberish or repeating words or sentences. Let your thoughts surprise you.

Do that now, before going on.

DO YOUR FIRST DISCOVERY WRITING ON AN INNOCUOUS TOPIC

The second step of this is a slight variation on what you just did. You will be doing real Discovery Writing but on a totally innocuous topic. The only way Discovery Writing is different from Stream-of-Consciousness Writing is that it is more directed, because you direct your mind to think about a certain topic and write down only the thoughts related to that.

I always have people do their first Discovery Writing on something that doesn't matter to them, because otherwise their heavy thoughts and feelings about the topic can interfere with learning the process. Once you see that you can do the process then you can use it on anything that matters to you.

Take a fresh sheet of lined paper and number down the left margin from 1 to 20. At the top margin write "20 THINGS THAT FLY." Now, *as fast as you can write*, list 20 things that fly — any twenty things that "fly" in any sense of the word. Doing it as fast as possible is very important, because this prevents the judgmental part of your mind from having time to work. Even if the judgmental part of your mind does tell you it doesn't like one, just write it down anyway and then write down the next one. No matter what, don't take more than three minutes to complete the entire list of 20.

Write that list now, before going on.

USING DISCOVERY WRITING ON SOMETHING THAT MATTERS TO YOU

Next I want you to write a Discovery List that is of practical value, so that you can see why I'm having you do this.

Again, don't take any longer than 3 minutes to complete the entire list of 20. *If you do this slowly you just won't get the desired result.* This is one of the few endeavors in life where speed counts for more than quality. Remember, the sole purpose of this is to get a creative flow of ideas. It is absolutely better to write the list fast and have a list of 20 of the stupidest ideas of all time than it is to write the list slowly and deliberately and write a list of 20 great ideas. Even if that seems bizarre, wrong, and difficult to you, try it anyway.

Very often people will think of one possible way of doing something, decide it won't work, then get frustrated and stop. If you list 99 bad ideas and one good idea, that's great! There will be plenty of time for passing judgment after you're done Discovery Writing.

Take another fresh sheet of paper, number from 1 to 20 and at the top write "20 THINGS I COULD DO TO INCREASE MY INCOME." Underline the word "could" twice to emphasize that you don't have to do any of these things. If you tell yourself that you're going to choose the best idea from the list and make yourself do it, then the judgmental part of your mind will kill your ideas. It's premature to be thinking about doing any of these. Just write all your ideas down as fast as you can. If an idea seems silly, write it down anyway and then write down the next one. Don't let your pen stop writing, even for a second.

Write that Discovery List now, and then I'll tell you some more using this method.

With practice you can get to where you can write a Discovery List of twenty of anything in two minutes. This is an excellent goal.

When you have completed the Discovery Writing look back over the list to see what you can learn from it. It is always best not to tell yourself that you are going to pick the best idea from the list and make yourself do it. Instead just see what you can learn.

Make Discovery Writing a daily habit. There is no self-improvement process that can produce as much result with as little investment of time as this. If you write a Discovery List of 20 ways you could increase your income every day for a month, it is almost impossible for your income not to go up. Indeed I have never known of even one person who has written a Discovery List of 20 ways to increase income every day for a month whose income did not go up as a direct result. In nine years of working with people to help them increase their prosperity, I have never seen anything else work as effectively as this.

Because creativity is the solution to every problem, when people start engaging their creativity in improving their lives, the results are profound and dramatic. One good idea can transform your entire life!

The scope of what you can do with this simple method is astonishing, because you can write Discovery Lists of anything. At the end of this chapter I'm going to suggest some special applications that I have found especially useful in my work with clients and seminar students over the years. Obviously you can make up your own. You can incorporate this technique into any kind of project that you are working on; you can use it to improve any aspect of your life. You can even write a Discovery List of Discovery Lists you could write!

Most people also find Discovery Writing to be quite enjoyable. It's fun seeing what your mind comes up with! It's a refreshing change of pace from analytical thinking, repetitive work or passive entertainment, like watching TV. Because it's so fast and varied, it never gets boring.

It only takes 1 to 3 minutes. You can do it anywhere. All you need is a piece of paper and something to write with. The only other thing you need is the gray matter between those enviable ears of yours.

Another benefit of this technique is that you will not only get ideas related to whatever your lists are about, you will also find your creativity increasing in general, too. After doing this every day for just a couple of weeks, you'll find yourself naturally thinking of solutions in situations where used to give up. You'll find yourself being more spontaneous at parties. Your sense of humor will improve. You'll be flooded with good ideas all the time. If you already spend a lot of your time on creative activities like writing or composing, etc., you'll find these things naturally going more smoothly, with less effort to get the ideas you are trying for. All of this will improve your self-esteem and you'll be happier than ever!

Yet another important benefit of Discovery Writing is that it greatly facilitates you in getting to know yourself. You really get to find out how your mind thinks. Some of the ideas that come up that don't really seem like very good ideas will still be very useful to you simply because it will be useful to find that your mind thinks that way. In some cases you will discover from this that you want to change your way of thinking. Chapter 14 on Attitude Builders will help you to do so.

Throughout the rest of this book we will be using Discovery Writing and variations on the general theme again and again. In some sections it will be used as a technique of self-discovery and in others as a reprogramming technique to help you change unwanted attitudes. These uses are in addition to its most fundamental use as a source of new, creative ideas.

Here is a summary of how to do Discovery Writing and some tips to make Discovery Writing work as well for yourself as possible:

1. Write what you are trying to accomplish on the top line of a sheet of lined paper.

2. Number down the left margin of your paper from 1 to 10 or from 1 to 20, first, before starting to list. Always make the list longer than you think is reasonable. In a very important sense, *it is easier to come up with twenty ideas than it is to come up with one.* You want to create a flow of ideas. One idea is not a flow. Two ideas are not usually enough and neither are five. But if you list ten ideas when you thought it would be hard to find even one, then you have a good creative flow operating and you greatly increase your chances of creating the idea you want. If this concept doesn't make sense to you, try the technique for a while and I think experience will convince you. This concept is related to a martial arts principle: you can break through an obstacle much more easily if you focus your mind past the obstacle than if you focus your mind on the obstacle.

3. Write the Discovery List as fast as you can. If it takes you more than three minutes to write your list of 20, even in the beginning, you are not really doing the process right — don't think so much and don't take it so seriously.

4. Do not pass judgment on any of the ideas until your entire Discovery List is completed.

5. Don't let your pen stop. Speedwriting is ideal. The idea is to "channel" ideas directly from your unconscious mind onto the paper. Speed helps greatly with this. Before you can pass judgment on the idea you just wrote down, write the next idea down and then the next.

6. Relax. Avoid pressuring yourself. Do not demand that your mind give you the correct solution. Just go for putting ideas and words

into new combinations. Give yourself as many different options as you can.

7. Do not plan on picking the best idea of the 20 and then putting that idea into action. For example, you are much better off making a list of 20 things you could do to increase your income with no particular intention of actually doing any of them, than you are making the list while telling yourself that you are going to pick the best one and put it into immediate action. The reason for this is that if you tell yourself you're going to put the best idea into action, the whole time you'll be passing judgment on whether you really want to do each one of them, which will defeat your purpose. Creativity is a function of freedom and spontaneity, not a function of discipline. If you make it completely fine with you to create a list of 20 stupid, childish, impractical ideas, you will strike a gold mine of excellent, workable ideas. The best ideas on your list will inspire you to action without your having to force yourself. If you're having to force yourself to take action on an idea, then you haven't found the right idea yet; go back to listing, without pressure.

8. When you are working on improving some area of your life, write a Discovery List about that once or twice every day until you get the result you want. It is OK if some of the same ideas come up each day for several days in a row. The best thing to do is to just write the list as fast as you can each day with whatever comes to mind, giving no attention at all to whether an idea came up yesterday.

9. You will find that this process works fine whether you are mentally alert or not; it is fine to do your daily listing when you first wake up and are still feeling groggy or when you are just about to go to bed and are feeling sleepy or any other time.

10. You can keep your lists in a notebook, for periodic review and inspiration. I do most of my listing on my computer and simply delete the ideas I don't like, so over a period of time I wind up with a long list of great ideas!

11. Since the process only takes 3 minutes at most, if your mind ever tells you that you don't have time to do your Discovery Writing, laugh, guffaw and howl in appreciation at that hilarious comedian you carry around with you in your head!

12. Most likely you'll find this process working almost perfectly right away. If you have trouble with it in any way at all, just keep trying. Reading the rest of this book will help, too.

SPECIAL APPLICATIONS OF DISCOVERY WRITING

Obviously you can apply Discovery Writing to absolutely any area of your life. There are four special applications that I want to address because I have helped so many people use Discovery Writing for these things: money, your love life, your health, and to help with creative writing.

"You've got to admit we look good together."

Drawing by Koren; © 1980 New Yorker Magazine, Inc.

CREATIVITY AND MONEY

The solution to any kind of financial problem lies in creativity. People usually think that money itself is the solution to money problems. It isn't. This is true because once you have solved the problem with the money, then you don't have that money for the next problem. Your creativity is available in infinite supply, however. If you know how to increase your income that is more valuable than any amount of money — just as it is more valuable to know how to get fish than it is to have any amount of fish.

Try these lists and make up your own:

20 THINGS I COULD DO TO INCREASE MY INCOME.

This is the list I give for homework to anyone who complains to me about not making enough money. I've never known of anyone doing this every day for a month whose income didn't go up as a result.

A variation, for those who are self-employed or engaged in commission sales is:

20 THINGS I COULD DO TO INCREASE SALES.

Or:

20 THINGS I COULD DO TO MEET NEW CUSTOMERS.

You can also use creativity at the opposite end:

20 THINGS I COULD DO TO REDUCE EXPENSES.

Or the combined effect:

20 THINGS I COULD DO TO INCREASE MY PROFITS.

Or:

20 THINGS I COULD DO TO INCREASE MY NET WORTH

If you have some kind of immediate pressing problem you can apply the technique very specifically. For instance, suppose your rent is due on the first and it looks like you're going to have a $500 shortfall:

20 THINGS I COULD DO IT RAISE $500 BY THE 1ST.

You don't always have to write a list of a specific number of items. For some kinds of lists it serves you to list everything you can think of.

For instance, suppose you don't like what you do for a living and you know you want to go into some other kind of work but you're not sure what. You can write a list of:

ALL THE CHARACTERISTICS OF MY IDEAL WAY OF MAKING A LIVING.

For example:

Makes me at least $2000 a month

Supports my purpose in life

Enables me to work with people I like

Allows me to wear nice clothes but doesn't require me to do so.

Then you could write a Discovery List of:

20 THINGS I COULD DO FOR A LIVING.

Then compare each item to your list of characteristics to help you choose.

Or suppose you know you want to invest your money in something, but you feel bewildered by what kind of investment to choose. Then write a Discovery List a list of:

ALL THE CHARACTERISTICS OF MY IDEAL INVESTMENT.

For example:

Very safe

Gives me an income every month

Doesn't require much time from me

or whatever.

Suppose you know you need to manage your spending better. You might as well start with:

ALL THE CHARACTERISTICS OF MY IDEAL BUDGET.

Then you could write a Discovery List of:

20 WAYS I COULD BUDGET MY MONEY.

Suppose you want to be wealthy but you wonder if you're the kind of person who is able to accomplish such things. Then write a Discovery List of:

20 THINGS ABOUT ME THAT SUPPORT MY BECOMING A MILLIONAIRE

You can use Discovery Writing to set goals, and in fact, in Chapter 8, you'll do just that.

If you already know what you are trying to accomplish but you feel helpless or bewildered, Chapter 5, will show you a series of Discovery Writings you can make to find the solution to any problem and the way to proceed with any task.

CREATIVITY AND YOUR LOVE LIFE

You can use Discovery Writing in quite a number of ways to help you with your love life.

For example, suppose you simply are looking for the right person to share your love life with. Then make this list:

ALL THE CHARACTERISTICS OF MY IDEAL LOVER (OR HUSBAND OR WIFE).

Once you've done that will at least be able to recognize the person if she or he comes along. You can compare everybody you know to the list and you might find out that you already know the person and simply hadn't recognized him or her for who she or he was! This happens more often than you might expect.

That list is how I met my former wife, Anne. I made my list and Anne came along three days later and we sat down together and checked off almost every item on the list. A long, productive and mostly satisfying relationship was the result.

You could even write a Discovery List of:

ALL THE AVAILABLE (WO)MEN I KNOW.

If it doesn't turn out to be anyone you already know, then you could write a Discovery List of:

20 WAYS I COULD MEET MY IDEAL LOVER (OR HUSBAND OR WIFE)

If you would like to do something new with someone try this list:

20 THINGS WE COULD DO ON A DATE

Variety is the spice of life. Want a little spice:

20 SEXY THINGS _____ AND I COULD DO.

If you are troubled in your love life by your low self-esteem, try:

20 THINGS ABOUT ME THAT MAKE ME ATTRACTIVE TO (WO)MEN

If you want just a general purpose toner-upper for your love life, then try:

20 THINGS I COULD DO TO IMPROVE MY LOVE LIFE.

CREATIVITY AND YOUR HEALTH

No matter how healthy or unhealthy you might be, there are things you could do to improve your health. What things? Try:

20 THINGS I COULD DO TO IMPROVE MY HEALTH

Maybe you have a pretty good sense of what to do but your not sure how to do it. You can try things like:

20 THINGS I COULD DO TO LOSE WEIGHT

Or:

20 THINGS I COULD DO THAT WOULD HELP ME QUIT SMOKING

Or:

20 THINGS I COULD DO THAT WOULD HELP ME STAY OFF DRUGS

Suppose you want to get more exercise but you've had trouble keeping up with exercise routines in the past. Then try:

20 ENJOYABLE PHYSICAL ACTIVITIES I COULD ENGAGE IN

Your main health problem might be that you have too much stress. Then try:

20 THINGS I COULD DO TO REDUCE MY STRESS

I found that list especially revealing.

Suppose you want to apply some structure to your diet for one reason or another. You can try:

ALL THE CHARACTERISTICS OF MY IDEAL DIET.

Or:

20 ENJOYABLE THINGS I COULD INCLUDE IN A DIET

If you are earnest about establishing mastery over your body, then try:

20 THINGS I COULD DO THAT WOULD SUPPORT ME IN MASTERING MY BODY.

At the very least it will be interesting to find out what your mind thinks!

If you've never thought about yourself as the kind of person who achieves true body mastery then write:

20 THINGS ABOUT ME THAT SUPPORT ME IN MASTERING MY BODY

HOW TO USE DISCOVERY WRITING TO HELP YOU WITH CREATIVE WRITING

Especially if you make your living by writing or doing some other creative sort of activity, some of the time you may find yourself feeling dry for new ideas. Instead of using whiskey or diet pills to help you get over your block try Discovery Writing! In all honesty, I know a lot more about writing than I do about painting or composing. I'll give you the lists I find helpful in writing and perhaps they can at least stimulate some ideas for non-verbal creative projects, too.

20 THINGS I COULD NAME MY MAIN CHARACTER.

ALL THE PERSONALITY TRAITS OF THIS CHARACTER.

20 THINGS THAT THIS CHARACTER MIGHT DO.

20 THINGS THAT COULD GO WRONG WITH THIS CHARACTER'S PLAN.

20 SOLUTIONS THIS CHARACTER MIGHT FIND TO HIS PROBLEM.
20 THINGS THAT COULD HAPPEN NEXT.
20 POSSIBLE THEMES FOR THIS EPISODE
20 WORDS I COULD USE INSTEAD OF . . .

It also works quite well to use simple Stream-of-Consciousness Writing, especially if you don't know at all what you want to write about.

I greatly prefer to write on a computer. I start virtually every writing project by just listing out all my ideas first in whatever order they come to mind. Then, using the word-processor I can move things around to the right order, delete ones that duplicate or that I don't think I'll use, etc. I can easily create an outline in this way. Then it's a simple matter to go to each item in the outline and flesh it out into the actual writing.

It's always best to separate writing from editing as much as possible. We were all taught in first grade to combine them, and write it out right the first time. That is really awful. Nobody can really write well that way. Mark Twain said, "If we were taught to talk in the same way that we were taught to write then all of us would stutter." A word processor is the ideal way to separate the writing from the editing. I find that I don't need to be nearly so clear-minded to be productive writing at a computer as I did when I used to write on a typewriter. This enables me to be productive during more of the day.

Nowadays, with excellent computers so inexpensive and word-processors so user-friendly, there is really no reason for any writer to have to put up with typewriters, scissors and Scotch tape. Using Discovery Writing as an aid to writing will work fine without a computer, but a computer is really the ideal medium for this application of Discovery Writing.

In summary, I want to encourage you again to try this technique out, on a number of topics, every day for a while. If you make this a daily practice, miracles will happen in your life. Anyway, it only takes a few minutes, so what have you got to lose?

CHAPTER 5

HOW TO USE DISCOVERY WRITING TO ACHIEVE ANY GOAL

In the previous chapter I presented a method, called Discovery Writing, for gaining reliable access to the creative flow. I also presented numerous examples of the kinds of things you can use it for.

In this chapter I present a single process that can be used for reliably achieving a creative breakthrough in any field of endeavor. When confronted by a problem or when embarking on a new project, (very nearly) the first thing one needs to do is answer the question, how best shall I proceed? This process will give you the answer to that question very quickly and with nearly absolute reliability.

The process consists of writing twenty Discovery lists of ten items each. Each list is designed to give you a different kind of insight, idea, or creative breakthrough. All you need to know at the start is what you are trying to accomplish. The process will do the rest, even if you start out in total bewilderment about how to accomplish your goal. In other words, by the end of the process you will have a good idea how best to proceed.

Use this process creatively. The breakthroughs and ideas might come at any point in the process. The processes are presented in an order that makes sense. In general I suggest simply starting at the beginning and making the lists in order. However, sometimes you might want to skip around, do more than 10 of one that seems to be a rich vein of breakthroughs, add your own steps, etc.

Don't give up, especially if the problem seems difficult. Also don't assume that a certain list is inapplicable or unlikely to produce anything for what you are working on. It only takes 1-2 minutes for each list anyway (about 30 to 40 minutes for the entire exercise) so try them all.

BE SURE TO STATE YOUR GOAL VERY CLEARLY AND PRECISELY!

1. Write a Discovery List of 10 possible ways to achieve this goal.

This is obviously a good place to start.

2. Write a Discovery List of 10 difficulties you might encounter in achieving this goal.

Making it finite and getting it down on paper can be a large help. Sometimes you can solve a problem simply by finding out that what has been running your mind is ridiculous.

3. Write a Discovery List of 10 things you know about achieving this goal.

This also includes things that you think you know. Include the obvious. Let your mind surprise you.

4. Write a Discovery List of 10 unknowns related to your achieving this goal.

Get the mysteries down on paper. They won't seem so overwhelming once you see that there are only a few. Put them down in any sort of wording at all. Don't worry about being "positive" with this list.

5. Write a Discovery List of 10 ways you could obtain more information about achieving this goal.

This includes both "internal" and "external" resources — figuring out, trying experiments, asking questions, reading books about it, etc.

6. Write a Discovery List of 10 resources you have that will help you achieve this goal.

Include every kind of resource: personal, mental, financial, social, etc. Anything that might help you with this project.

7. Write a Discovery List of 10 related things you have done before.

Even if they are only distantly related. They could be very specific or as general as "I've dealt with people before," or "I've solved financial problems before," or "I've solved difficult problems before."

8. Write a Discovery List of 10 apparent restrictions on how you can proceed.

These might all start with "I must." Include the obvious.

9. Write a Discovery List of 10 ways that the process of achieving this goal might turn out to be different from how it now appears.

Solutions almost always turn out to be different than initial assumptions. You'll be amazed at how much insight your mind already has on this if you just give it a context for expressing itself to you.

10. Write a Discovery List of 10 things you hope to accomplish by achieving this goal.

Just write down the things that are motivating you to be pursuing this at all. Let the silly, selfish or even the embarrassing ones come out onto paper. By being as clear as possible on this you may discover a way to bypass your anticipated difficulties.

11. Write a Discovery List of 10 new ways of stating your goal.

Often apparent limitations are just a result of the way you are thinking. By trying out other ways to describe the same goal, important breakthroughs commonly occur. What is it that you really want?

12. Write a Discovery List of 10 ways you could take shortcuts to get what you want in this.

Sometimes an easier way may be staring you in the face. Remember, stay fixed on the goal but be flexible about the method.

13. Draw 10 different, simple pictures of it.

Engaging the visual part of your mind reveals something new. You don't need to be an artist to do this. Just doodle little stuff and see what comes up. If nothing comes up, doodle anyway. Be open to getting a new perspective in this way.

14. Write a Discovery List of 10 separate steps the project could be broken down into.

© 1989 David Sippress

Reprinted by permission.

The list doesn't have to be in order and the steps don't even have to be of the same magnitude. (List any intermediate steps in any order that they come to mind.)

15. Write a Discovery List of 10 ways other people could assist you in achieving this goal.

List both the obvious and the apparently impossible.

16. Write a Discovery List of 10 people who could be useful to you in achieving this goal.

On this list you can put both specific names and/or general descriptions (e.g., "a psychologist," "the reference librarian," "my customers," etc.)

17. Write a Discovery List of 10 things you might find undesirable about achieving this goal.

This is one of the most important of these Lists, even if it brings up uncomfortable feelings. When writing this List, concern yourself not with being positive, but only with being honest. If your mind tells you that you don't find *anything* undesirable about your goal, then write down what you *would* find undesirable about it if you *did*. Inviting your unconscious mind to share this material with you can be helpful to you in many different ways.

18. Write a Discovery List of 10 ways in which achieving this goal fits in with your personal values.

Knowing this will help you with motivation and give you additional insights into fitting your project into your life.

19. Write a Discovery List of 10 positive thoughts or affirmations that could help you achieve this goal.

An affirmation inventory can be an enormous asset in solving any kind of problem. Often the affirmation begins to work as soon as you think it up. See Chapter 14 for detailed information about affirmations.

20. Write a Discovery List of 10 productive things you could do immediately to move you toward achieving this goal.

"The journey of a thousand miles begins with a single step." Even if these are very simple things, you may get both conceptual and emotional breakthroughs with these.Sometimes you can get a creative breakthrough better when you are working on the project even if you think what you can do will be inadequate.

Having done this process you very probably have a much better idea of how to proceed. Use this process frequently to keep your creativity flowing and your resourcefulness in top shape.

Note: At a very reasonable cost we will send you the entire process presented in this chapter in a format that is very convenient for use. It is neatly typeset and printed with lines for your Discovery Writing and blank space for the drawing exercise, stapled together on ten pages, with a front page of instructions. It is highly suitable both for individual use and for use in groups. See the Materials Appendix.

PART II

FROM POTENTIAL
TO FULFILLMENT

From reading Part I of this book you have acquired several important skills. You have learned how to cultivate the qualities of creativity so that all parts of your life can be supportive of your creative endeavors.

You have learned how to tap your infinite wellspring of creativity and how to put that to practical use for solving problems and figuring out how best to achieve goals.

Important questions now arise for you to ask yourself: What do I most want to accomplish? How best can I be of service to humankind? What projects would be best for me to work on? What would be the best use of my time and energy? How best can I go from having infinite creative potential to maximizing my fulfillment as a human being?

Part II of this book addresses these questions.

Before you can do any good in your life or any good in the world you need to become as clear as possible on what exactly "good" means to you, i.e., what your values are. Chapter 6, "Your Motivation and Your Values," enables you to find out exactly what your values are and how they motivate you. The Values Process, in this chapter, is a better tool for getting to know your mind than any other that I know of.

The biggest question to which any human being can address himself is "What is the purpose of my life?" All other questions about your life are meaningless without first answering this one. Indeed, if you don't know your purpose in life my best suggestion is: *Cease all activity at once and don't start doing anything again until you do know what your purpose in life is.* Fortunately it is easy to discover your purpose in life; Chapter 7 tells you all about it.

Once you know your values and your purpose in life you can set goals that will be meaningful to you. Without knowing your values and your purpose in life any goals you set will not be truly your goals — they'll be the goals your parents or your friends or the leader of some group you belong to think you should have. If they aren't truly your goals you'll always think they should motivate you but they won't. Follow the instructions in Chapter 8 and emerge with a very clear idea of where you want your life to go.

Once you have chosen meaningful goals you are going to need some planning. The Creative Time Management System, presented in Chapter 9 is the simplest, most economical, most practical system of activity coordination I have ever seen. It is so straightforward that it is hard to imagine how any time management system could be any better — it is everything you need for coordinating all parts of your life — and nothing you don't need.

Part II finishes with some simple suggestions for creating your own custom-designed money management system.

By following the instructions in Part II of this book you can start wherever you are now and wind up with the most fulfilling life you could possibly lead.

CHAPTER 6

YOUR MOTIVATION AND YOUR VALUES

This chapter about why you do what you do — your motivations.
"What you do" is called your behavior. Your behavior includes
everything that you do under any circumstances. All the diverse,
specific activities that you engage are what I shall call your individual
behaviors. Your behaviors are not the things you wish you did, nor
the things that you like to tell yourself you do, nor are they the

85

activities that it would be best for you to do to achieve your goals — they are the things that you actually do.

Every behavior has at least one motivation, many times several. The motivation is the inner force that moves you. In some uses of the word "motivation," people speak of one person being more motivated than another, or of sometimes feeling "a lack of motivation." That is not how I am using the word. The way I am using the word, a workaholic and someone who just lies around on the couch all day are equally motivated — they are just motivated to do different things.

Not all people who engage in the same behaviors have the same motivations and not all people who have the same motivations engage in the same behaviors. For example one person who lies around all day may be motivated by a desire to fail in order to get even with pushy parents while another may lie around all day because of fear of failure, thus never attempting to do anything. But a workaholic can also be motivated by fear of failure, thus working hard all the time to avoid it, or by a desire to get even with pushy parents by surpassing their accomplishments.

All of us are sometimes motivated by things we know about (conscious motivation) and sometimes by things we don't know about (unconscious motivation). Usually our behaviors are motivated by a combination of both. For example a person's conscious motivation for eating something might be just to find out what it tastes like while the unconscious motivation might be to suppress a feeling, such as loneliness or boredom. For our purposes here we don't need to explore why we are sometimes motivated consciously and sometimes unconsciously, it is sufficient simply to note that both things happen.

All motivation, whether conscious or unconscious, comes from values. By "values" I mean the qualities or things that you have decided are valuable for you. A value is what you think is valuable for its own sake. Whenever you value anything you are motivated to increase your experience of that. For example, if you value money then you have motivation to increase your experience of money. If you value love then you have motivation to increase your experience of love. Similarly, you may value the absence of something, such as discomfort.

In most cases the words "motivation" and "desire" can be used interchangeably. Most correctly, you have a desire for what you value and the desire motivates you to engage in behaviors intended to get you more of that.

As you go through life your mind automatically seeks better and better ways to give you more of what you like and less of what you don't like. Obviously some of your mind's strategies don't work; these provide learning opportunities and motivation to try something different next time. Sometimes, however, you may find yourself habitually engaging in the same behavior over and over again even though you already know that it doesn't really work. Part III of this book will give you additional insight into why this happens and what to do about it.

Sometimes you have opposing sets of values that conflict with one another. For example, you may have a desire to be prosperous but also habitually find fault with prosperous people, thus creating a desire to be unlike them. This is a main source of financial self-sabotage for many struggling poor people. Or suppose you are married and you have both a desire for the social company of many people of the opposite sex and a desire for your spouse to not feel threatened (and the belief that he or she would feel threatened if you had many friends of the opposite sex). This is a common source of tension in marriages. Having conflicting values creates an internal power struggle, confusion, conflicting behaviors and self-sabotage.

One of the many advantages of developing a detailed knowledge of your own values is that it enables you to eliminate these problems of self-conflict. A simple, effective method for developing a detailed knowledge of your own values is presented toward the end of this chapter.

COMPULSION, DISCIPLINE AND ENTHUSIASM

There are three main modes of motivation: compulsion, discipline and enthusiasm. All three come from values. What sets them apart from one another is the relationship between conscious motivation and unconscious motivation.

Compulsion means unconsciously motivated desires controlling behavior against the will of the conscious mind. A simple example is alcoholism. All alcoholics can see that the way they are drinking is devastating their lives and all alcoholics try to control their drinking. But their compulsion is stronger than their conscious will and they continue engaging in the destructive behavior. There are many, many less obvious examples and everyone engages in compulsive behavior to some extent.

Discipline means the conscious mind's controlling one's behavior despite opposing desires in the unconscious mind. Anyone who has ever worked at a boring job has experienced this — strong urges to do something else but disciplining oneself to keep working anyway and wait until it's OK with the boss to do something else. It is important to have a certain amount of discipline but it can have serious drawbacks, too.

Enthusiasm means that the conscious mind's values and the unconscious mind's values are in alignment, working together harmoniously. Enthusiasm is by far the best mode of motivation. When you are enthusiastic it is easy to stay on purpose with whatever you are working on. You feel happy and you don't have to contend constantly with wanting relief from emotional discomfort, as you do when operating from either compulsion or discipline. When you are feeling enthusiastic it is natural to be creative. In addition, other people sense your enthusiasm and naturally want to participate with you.

Not everything that seems at first to be enthusiasm really is. There is a certain manic phase in indulging a compulsion that can seem like enthusiasm at the time but really isn't. It involves the suppression of one's better judgment and of one's concerns about the consequences. Any time you think you are feeling enthusiastic but also think you may regret what you are doing later, you can be assured that what you are really experiencing is compulsion.

It is also possible to put on a front of enthusiasm when you are really engaging in discipline. This can feel like a roller-coaster ride of excessive activity followed by excessive stress, while all the time putting on a happy exterior. Certainly it is good to stay on purpose with your projects but it is also good to tend to the needs of your unconscious mind. If you learn to acknowledge these needs consciously you can probably find a way to take care of them and make your project go more smoothly, too.

Do not confuse discipline with enthusiastic diligence. True, in both cases one is earnest about one's work and tends to work for long periods without taking a break. Even so, it is easy to tell the difference between the two. What I am calling discipline (which could also be called "suppressive discipline" for clarity) doesn't feel good. It feels like forcing yourself. It feels like you can't wait until the goal is achieved so you can drop the disciplined program you've been on. It's a holdover from being disciplined by your parents and teachers — forced to do things their way. Enthusiastic diligence, on the other hand, feels wonderful. It feels like staying on purpose with your project even when potential distractions arise either in your own mind or in your environment. It feels like you are at choice, like you are so enthusiastic about the project you are working on that when an opportunity to stop working presents itself you naturally say "no thank you."

If you are doing what you are doing only to achieve the end result and you are disliking the process, then you are engaging in suppressive discipline. If you are both enjoying the process and looking forward to the result, and you find it easy and natural to stay on purpose, then you are engaging in enthusiastic diligence.

Although compulsion and discipline are in some ways opposites, they are somewhat alike. Compulsion and discipline both tend to be draining. Anyone who has ever experienced compulsion knows how draining it can be. Discipline is in many ways superior and certainly has a better reputation — almost anybody would rather have an excessively disciplined neighbor than a compulsive one. However, even when the results of one's disciplined activities are enlivening, the effort involved in resisting the urges of the unconscious mind creates a "slush fund" of suppressed emotion that reduces enthusiasm, happiness and self-esteem in the long run. One aspect of discipline is that you make what you're doing more important than your feelings. This is fine once in a while but is disempowering over the long run. Anyway, your emotions can be doorways to parts of your unconscious mind that you cannot gain easy access to in any other way. The most disciplined people are not usually the most creative.

I am not really arguing against discipline but in favor of enthusiasm. Discipline is OK and even necessary in its place. However, there are many who seek to fill their lives with discipline for its own sake. I assert that this is little better than compulsively avoiding discipline. I suggest that when you are looking for a solution to a problem in your behavior that you seek a change based on enthusiasm instead of one based on discipline. The reason diets don't work in the long run for losing weight is that no one is willing to deny one's desires forever. To cultivate enthusiasm for physical activities and for a healthy, beautiful body is far more effective in the long run than trying to use discipline to stay on a diet.

Neither compulsion nor discipline is bad, only less desirable than enthusiasm. To have no compulsion whatsoever would be tantamount to having no unconscious mind — I certainly don't know anybody who comes close to that. Given that situation, it is unrealistic to expect to accomplish very much good without some discipline. The purpose of discipline is to create certainty. A person with no discipline is a slave to unconscious desires.

Compulsion can be valuable, too, because the conscious mind can at times be prone to tangents. Almost everyone has times when the conscious mind forms a sudden and misguided new resolve and only the limits imposed by the unconscious mind avert disaster. Praise your mind for working as well as it does and you will get far better results than if you get negative about your negativity.

Fortunately there is a highly effective method of caring for the unconscious mind. It enables one to handle the underlying causes of compulsions and to be sensitive to the needs of the unconscious mind so that one doesn't burn out from excessive discipline. This method is called "Vivation" and is described in Chapter 12.

The more you feel enthusiastic the more you are in alignment with your purpose. Your purpose comes from your unique combination of skills and values. When you are using discipline and are not feeling enthusiastic, it is highly possible that at least some part of your plan is not in alignment with your purpose. Discipline in the face of this is a form of suppression — suppressing the feelings that come from having a flawed plan. Processing your mind in order to restore your enthusiasm is tantamount to improving your plan of action by making it a better reflection of who you really are.

Obviously it is highly desirable to know how to increase your enthusiasm at will. This means being able to be truthful with yourself about what is limiting your enthusiasm and being able to resolve internal conflicts.

The solution to all conflicts (internal or interpersonal) is to find the shared intentions of the conflicting parts and then focus on those shared intentions. When both parts realize that they are really wanting the same thing, they will cooperate in doing whatever is best to achieve that.

For example, suppose you are overweight and trying to diet but are craving chocolate cake. One part of you wants you to forget about food and the other part wants you to be self-indulgent. How many shared intentions can you think of? Here are three: 1. Both parts want you to enjoy your life more. 2. Both parts want you to focus all your attention on your mouth and your digestive organs. 3. Both parts want more love. Based on those examples, here are three solutions to that internal conflict, which could be applied either separately or together: 1. Focus immediately on enjoying this moment more, keep cultivating your focus on that and soon the internal conflict will disappear. 2. Specifically you can focus on the extent which the feelings in your mouth and digestive organs already do feel good. (Vivation, which is explained in Chapter 12, will help with this.) 3. Since both parts want love, initiate contact with someone who makes you feel loved. If you do that I'll bet your mind forgets all about chocolate cakes and diets.

There is no substitute for developing a detailed knowledge of your own values. When you have that detailed knowledge you will understand why you do what you do — this leads to a greater degree of compassion for yourself and to the resolution of internal conflicts.

THE VALUES PROCESS

Like everyone else you value some things more than others. Whenever you like something you, you like certain specific things about it. When you like a person, there are specific qualities about that person that you value especially much. These "likes" are your values. No two people have exactly the same values and yet you will naturally get along the best with those people who have values most similar to your own. There are some people who have values very, very different from yours; you will actually meet these people only rarely, however, because your lives will follow such different paths.

You do not give equal weight to all your values. You put them in a certain order of priorities. It is the priority order of your values that causes you to make the decisions that you do. For example, decisions like "shall I continue living in rural Oregon, near my family and friends, or shall I move to San Francisco where I can make more money." This is a weighing process whether it happens consciously or unconsciously. Some part of your mind has to determine whether it values living amidst old friends and family more or values improved economic prospects more. This kind of weighing even happens with simple decisions like which main course to choose at a restaurant.

Your values change with time, too. This is the main reason your life goes through different phases. As your values change, your decisions and your behaviors change and thus you bring different people and experiences into your life.

The Values Process will make clear your values and the relative priority you give them. It will give you detailed insight into your motivations. When you are done, if you have any patterns of behavior that you would like to change, you can do the process at the end of this chapter, and use these insights in a straightforward, self-directed behavior modification process.

The best way to do the Values Process is to use 100 or so blank cards. 3×5 cards are fine; blank business cards, which we use for many other processes in this book, are somewhat better, because they are smaller. (See the Materials Appendix for how to get blank business cards cheaply and quickly.)

The process is simple:

1. Count out 100 cards and have a rubber band handy to keep them together. You are going to write your values on these cards.

2. In your first session with the cards, write down twenty or so things that you value, one per card. They can be literally "things," your car for example, or people, or abstract qualities, such as love.

3. Then carry the cards around with you for a day or two. Every time you notice that you value something, right it down on a card. Sunsets, kitty cats, simplicity, truth, good public transportation, clean fresh air, or whatever you happen to notice and realize that you value.

Additionally, whenever you notice yourself finding fault with someone or something, that tells you that value the opposite, for example: if you go to a movie and find fault with it for being boring, that shows you that you value entertaining movies, or even the abstract quality of entertainment itself; if you read in the paper about someone committing a murder (certainly an easy thing to find fault with), that might tell you that you value several things, safety, people being kind to one another, law and order, etc. In each case write down on the card the "positive" thing that you do value, not the "negative" thing that you don't value. It works better to write down "comfort" than to write down "avoiding discomfort."

4. Keep doing this until you have written a value on each of the 100 cards. The process works best if you take at least 24 hours but no more than five days to complete all 100 cards.

5. When you have written a value on each of 100 cards, you are ready to begin the next stage of this process — putting your values in priority order. IMPORTANT: This does not mean the order that you like to think you value them — it means the order of priority that is indicated by your behavior. Here is how to proceed with putting them in order:

6. Read through all of the cards to familiarize yourself with them. In the course of this you may notice that some of your cards are so closely related to each other that they could be called one and the same. In this case you can eliminate one of them and keep only the one that is a better statement of what you are truly valuing. Be careful in this process, however, because some similar or related things may not be equivalent. For example "being married" and "being married to my present wife" may or may not be equivalent for you — that is for you to decide.

It is also OK to modify what you have written on the card somewhat to make it a better statement of what you truly value.

7. Now decide which twenty, out of all your cards, you value the very most.

This is your first experience in choosing one value over another and I acknowledge that it may seem both odd and difficult to you at first. Just do it anyway. Enjoy the weirdness of it. Enjoy the decisiveness. Even if you don't enjoy weirdness and decisiveness, just do it anyway.

When you have chosen the twenty cards you value the most, separate them from the rest. You could even throw the rest of them away and keep only the top twenty; the remainder of this process involves only those twenty chosen cards.

8. Put these twenty cards into order relative to each other, the card you value the most at the top and your "number-20" most valued card last. The reason cards are good for this process is that to put the cards into a stack at all you have to put them in some order.

Much of the time you may choose the more abstract card over the more specific card, for example, "being able to go where I want when I want" over "my car." This will almost certainly not be true all of the time however. For instance it may seem to you that even though you value being married to your present wife, if you separated from her you probably would not choose to remarry. That might mean that you value the more specific "being married to my present wife" over the more abstract "being married."

9. Now test that order by taking the top two (which we can call "a" and "b") and saying to yourself "My behavior indicates that I value "____" (Card A) more than "_____" (Card B). Check out whether it feels true. To help with this you can imagine a hypothetical case where you would have to choose between those two, or remember a real time that such a choice had to be made in the past. If the

93

statement seems true, then leave card "a" in first place and then compare cards "b" and "c" in the same way. If it doesn't seem true, then switch the order of "a" and "b" and go on to compare the former card "a" with card "c," etc. Go through all twenty in this way, more than once if necessary, until you are confident that all twenty cards are indeed in the order that your behavior indicates you value them.

That completes this process, although there is a lot you can do with the results of this, which I shall explain.

© 1989, BLOOM COUNTY by Berke Breathed
Washington Post Writers Group Reprinted with permission

HOW TO INTERPRET THE RESULTS OF THE VALUES PROCESS

You will almost certainly be surprised at what comes from this process. You might even be shocked or upset if you really do it honestly (which is certainly the way to do it). You may find out that there are important differences between how you are, as revealed by doing this process, and how you have always thought you were. You may find out that your mind is not really set up on the same logic as you had believed it was. You may find out things like why you are an overeater, why you have never made the leap to self-employment, why you have never gotten along with a particular co-worker, etc.

Look over the order of your cards several times and let your mind play around with what the cards tell you. Think about the various problems you have in your life. Think about the patterns of behavior that you like and the patterns you don't like. Let the cards give you insight.

Think about how your life would be different if your values had a different priority. Go through the cards and as you contemplate each one think about the effect it would have on you if you valued each one less or a lot less, more or a lot more. Play a game of what-if with yourself.

Consider specific pairs of cards and what would happen if you changed the order of them relative to each other. "What if I valued my health more than comfort? Would I exercise more?" "What if I valued freedom more than security? Would I quit my job? Would I stay married?" "If I valued money more than convenience would I cook at home more and eat out less?"

I suggest doing this process every three to six months. Keep your 20 cards, in order, from each time you do it, somewhere where you can find them. After completing the process each time compare your cards to the last time you did it. You will be amazed at the insight it gives you into the ways you have changed. This process conveys insight into how one has changed over time better than anything else I have ever seen. You'll find that some priorities have stayed about the same and others have changed quite a lot — as you change and evolve it is reflected clearly in your values. It really is one of the very best ways to stay in touch with yourself.

SPECIAL APPLICATIONS OF THE VALUES PROCESS

You can use your knowledge of your values to help you make many kinds of decisions. For example, in Chapter 8 we will be using your results from this process to help you decide which goals are really the most meaningful for you, i.e., what direction for your life will lead to the greatest fulfillment for you.

Detailed knowledge of your values will help you in making every kind of decision, both large and small. It can help you decide what kind of car to buy. It can help you decide what kind of investment to make. It can help you decide whether you are likely to really use a new piece of exercise equipment or not. it can even help you decide what kind of image to project, how to wear your hair, what clothes to buy! Really it can help you with every kind of decision. Any decision made in accord with your own values and priorities is certain to work out better than any decision based on whim or on the opinions of other people.

If you ever do this process with a friend, lover, business associate or spouse and then compare values at the end, you will find the differences between you, as revealed by the process, very interesting! You'll be amazed at the insight it gives you into your relationship with that person.

Friendships, loving relationships, business partnerships, etc., can work only when there is a strong alignment of values. Certainly not all the values need to be the same or match up well, but if they are very, very different you can depend on there being conflict. This process will show the conflicts, and their causes, very clearly.

A SELF-IMPROVEMENT METHOD OF BEHAVIOR MODIFICATION

This process uses the insights you gained from doing the Values Process.

This process is useful if you are not entirely pleased with your behavior, or to say the same thing differently, with the priorities that you give your values.

Values motivate you according to the relative priority that you give them. For example, if you value security more than freedom, then you may stay in your current job, even if you don't like it, rather than look for a better job or become self-employed. Another example is that if you are an overeater or a cigarette smoker that means that you value emotional comfort more than you value health.

Think about what the cards tell you about possible solutions to some of your problems. It is possible, through a simple self-improvement technique, to change the priority you give your values and have your behavior change dramatically as a result. Ask yourself, "Is there anything about my behavior or my priorities that it would serve me to change?"

The method for changing your priority of values, and your behavior, involves a special application of affirmations, which are an advanced self-improvement concept explained in greater detail in Chapter 14.

Here are the steps to working this process. An example, to make it clearer, follows immediately after the instructions.

1. Identify the problem behavior.

2. Identify which specific order of values motivate that behavior.

3. Create an affirmation in the following way: "_____ is more important to me than _____." In the first blank put the value of lower priority. In the second blank put the value of higher priority. Follow the instructions for using affirmations presented in Chapter 14.

Do this every day, or twice a day if your prefer, until the behavior changes.

Example of using the self-improvement behavior modification method:

Imagine, if you will, a young woman whom we'll call "Thelma" who does the Values Process.

Thelma's 20 values, in order, are these:

1 Love
2 Having enough money
3 Having a good job
4 Having a man
5 Food
6 Sex
7 My car
8 Living in a nice apartment
9 Entertainment
10 My friends
11 Rock concerts
12 Emotional comfort
13 My health
14 The approval of my family
15 My pet cat
16 Travel

17 Expressing myself
18 Going to seminars
19 Working out at the spa
20 Paying off my credit card every month

Now suppose it has always bothered Thelma that she puts on an act when she's around her family. She doesn't tell them what's really going on in her life. She doesn't comment on how her father's drinking worries her. And she especially doesn't tell how much she resents the inappropriate advice they all give her.

Step 1. "I don't express myself around my family."

Step 2. There are two of these: A. Valuing emotional comfort more than expressing myself. B. Valuing the approval of my family more than expressing myself. Either of these could be used for modifying this problem but Thelma figures that if she chooses "emotional comfort" she will handle this problem and some others as well.

Step 3. Expressing myself is more important than my emotional comfort from now on.

*Expressing myself is more important than my emotional comfort.
(No, because I'll never have emotional comfort again)
*Expressing myself obviously supports my emotional comfort.
Expressing myself is more important than my emotional comfort.
(No, because everyone will hate me.)
*Obviously everyone likes me more than ever now that I express my true thoughts and feelings.
Expressing myself is more important than my emotional comfort.
(My father will never speak to me again)
*Now that I communicate more honestly with my father, my father communicates more honestly with me.
Thelma, expressing yourself is more important than your emotional comfort.
(I'm not that courageous)
*Obviously I am more than courageous enough to express my honest thoughts and feelings.
Thelma, expressing yourself is more important than your emotional comfort.
(I can't do it)
*Expressing myself honestly feels completely natural now.
Thelma, expressing yourself is more important than your emotional comfort from now on.

(My friends will leave me)
*My friends like to be with me more than ever now that I am more expressive.
Expressing herself is more important for Thelma than her emotional comfort.
(I'll lose my job)
*Expressing myself obviously supports my career.
Expressing herself is more important for Thelma than her emotional comfort.
(The bitch!)
*Expressing myself obviously makes me a better person.
Expressing herself is more important for Thelma than her emotional comfort.
(It would be worth it)
*Obviously it is worth anything it takes to express myself.
Expressing myself is more important than my emotional comfort.

Thelma notices some change the first day and after a week she gets up the courage to call her mother and tell her things she has never told her before.

ADDITIONAL NOTES ON USING AFFIRMATIONS WITH THE VALUES PROCESS:

In some cases you might find that you are not pleased that you are motivated at all by certain values. For instance you may have discovered that you are motivated by selfishness. If this is not OK with you then you will suffer from internal conflict. My earnest and long-considered advice to you is to work with repetitions of an affirmation in the format "It is OK for me to be motivated by _____." For example, "it is OK for me to be motivated by selfishness." This will turn out entirely to your benefit regardless of your opinion of selfishness.

Sometimes you might be pleased both by your motivation by your values and by their relative priority, but not by their apparent conflict. In that case you can use an affirmation in the format "My _____ contributes to my _____ and my _____ contributes to my _____. In you put one of the conflicting values in the first and fourth blanks and the other in the second and third blanks. For example, "My freedom contributes to my security and my security contributes to my freedom."

I also want to point out that Chapter 14 has tips on more advanced methods for working with affirmations than what I just showed you here and you can use any of those methods with these same basic ideas, too.

CONCLUSION

I have described many specific benefits of knowing your own values in a detailed way. In addition you will also find many of your own because of one major general benefit: If you know what you want you are a lot more likely to get it and a lot more likely to recognize it when it shows up.

CHAPTER 7

YOUR PURPOSE IN LIFE

For all us humans, knowing the purpose of our lives is the most important existential need.

Because you are unique, having knowledge, background, values and ambitions unlike anyone else's, your purpose is also unique. Your purpose represents the unique contribution to the world that only you can make. Your purpose is your path of greatest personal fulfillment.

Knowing your purpose gives you a sense of direction, a guiding star by which to navigate your life. It allows you to set goals for your journey, measure your progress and make corrections as necessary. It will be a beacon of inspiration to you in life's darker moments. Once you know your purpose, nothing can ever take it away from you.

If you do not know your purpose then your life will be guided primarily by other people's purposes for you. Almost everyone can find some use for you. If you don't know your own purpose, then when people try to make you fit into roles that suit their needs you will tend to go along, because any purpose is better than none. This means working at jobs that have nothing to do with who you are, relationship roles that aren't fulfilling, and patterns of low self-esteem that permeate your entire experience of life.

Without a sense of your own purpose you have two alternatives, conformity or rebelliousness. Conformity means doing what other people want you to do. Rebelliousness means doing the opposite of what other people want you to do. There is absolutely no fulfillment in either one of these. Conformists generally have more security but they don't learn as much about life as rebels do, because they don't question. Rebels like to think they have more freedom but really they don't at all. Since they do the opposite of what people want them to do, they think other people don't control them; really the life of a rebel is determined by the values of others every bit as much as is that of the conformist because all the motivation still comes from outside. All the existential dilemmas remain.

There is an alternative to rebelliousness and conformity, however. That is self-directedness. A self-directed person knows his or her own purpose and does not look to other people for definition. A self-directed person is an initiator and a leader. Other people naturally align themselves to the self-directed person, to share in the purposefulness they find there. Only through self-directedness can fulfillment be found. The rebel and the conformist are always plagued by profound questions about whether they are doing the right thing with their lives — the self-directed person experiences certainty. Being a conformist or a rebel is like riding an inter-city bus — the best you can get is to be taken to somewhere near where you want to go, but you know you won't be taken right to your door. Being self-directed is like driving your own car — you can go exactly where you want when you want because you are in charge of your life.

It is very difficult to make any kind of big decision in a meaningful way without knowing your purpose. Compared to knowing what your purpose is, all other decisions are trivial. Your purpose is not something that you achieve once and are then done with, it is something for you to express continuously, giving meaning to goals throughout your life. Your purpose puts your entire life into perspective.

You can discover the purpose of your life through use of a simple process. Here, then, is the process for discovering your purpose:

THE PURPOSE PROCESS

1. Think about this: If you had the power to make the World be any way at all, how would you choose for it to be? Now write that down

© 1989, BLOOM COUNTY by Berke Breathed
Washington Post Writers Group Reprinted with permission

in 20 words or less. It is best for this to be stated entirely in positive language. For instance it is better to say "peace and prosperity for everyone" than to say "no war or poverty." We'll call this description your "ideal World."

2. Make a list of 10 things you like about yourself. (This will be a list of nouns: "my culinary skill, my intellect, my sense of humor," etc.) We'll call this "List 1."

3. Choose from List 1 the three things (or four) that are the most significant to you.

4. Make a list of 10 activities you enjoy engaging in as an expression of the three or four things you just chose. (Each item on this list will contain a gerund — a word ending in -ing, "cooking, reading, telling jokes," etc.) We'll call this "List 2."

5. Pick the four items (or three or five) from List 2 that make the biggest contribution to making the World more like the ideal World you just described.

6. Create your Statement of Purpose by writing out the following sentence, filling in the blanks as instructed: "My purpose is to use my _____, _____, and _____ by _____ing, ____ing, and _____ing so that _____."

Fill in the first set of blanks (between "my" and "by") with the three or four items you chose from List 1. Fill in the second set of blanks (between "by" and "so that") with the three or four items you chose from List 2. Fill in the last blank with your description of the ideal World. Now polish up the grammar so you get a good sentence.

Congratulations! You now know your purpose in life!

Here are a couple of additional tips on making this process work optimally:

1. Don't worry if your purpose doesn't come out seeming exactly right the first time you do it. That's normal. At first, I suggest that you do this process once a day for about a week. Then do it every few months forever. You'll probably find that the first few times you do it you get fairly different Statements of Purpose each time. After a while it will settle down and be almost the same every time.

2. You want the items in your Statement of Purpose to be specific enough to provide genuine guidance and abstract enough to apply to many goals over many years.

I'll share with you the Statement of Purpose that has guided me for several years now: "My purpose is to use my creativity, insight and communication skills by leading seminars, writing books and articles, and going on TV and radio, so that everyone enthusiastically serves everyone."

HOW TO USE YOUR STATEMENT OF PURPOSE

1. Write your Statement of Purpose neatly on a card and carry it with you in your purse or wallet. You can also put it on a sign in your home or work place where you will see it often.

2. Whenever you have a decision to make, ask yourself, which option will serve my purpose best?

3. Any time you are setting a goal make sure that the goal is an expression of your purpose. Any goal that is not an expression of your purpose will be unsatisfying even when you achieve it.

4. If you are working on a team of any kind (including marriage) have your team mates and potential team mates do this process and compare purposes so you can see if there is enough alignment of purpose for the team to work together well. It is also an excellent idea to formulate a statement of group purpose.

5. Let people know what your purpose is. Your purpose is something to be proud of. When people know what your purpose is they will know you better and trust and respect you more than they did before they knew your purpose. You can even include your Statement of Purpose on brochures, resumes and business cards.

SPECIAL APPLICATIONS OF THE PURPOSE PROCESS

Besides using the Purpose Process to discover the purpose of your life, you can also use it to discover the purpose of specific things that are part of your life. For example:

The purpose of your business:

1. Make a list of ten things you like that are characteristic of your business.

2. Pick the three (or four) most important.

3. Make a list of ten things your business does well as an expression of those chosen characteristics.

4. As before, describe the ideal World.

5. Pick the three (or four) activities of your business (list 2) that make the biggest contribution to creating the ideal World.

6. Write out the Statement of Purpose: "The purpose of (the name of your business) is to use our _____, _____, and _____ , by _____ ing, _____ ing, and _____ ing so that _____ ."

The purpose of International Vivation Community is to use our expert instructors, high values, and global campus by teaching Vivation, providing a community of support, and developing autonomous leaders so that everyone enthusiastically serves everyone.

Some other purposes I suggest investigating are:

The purpose of your love life.

The purpose of your marriage.

The purpose of your mind.

The purpose of your body.

Your ability to make the best use of anything is a function of your understanding of its purpose.

CHAPTER 8

WHAT ACCOMPLISHMENTS WOULD FULFILL YOU MOST?

Goals are milestones along the path of expressing your purpose. Without knowing your purpose in life, goals are meaningless. If you have not yet done the Purpose Process in Chapter 7, go back and do that process now, before going on with this chapter.

Goals are different from desires in that goals are more specific and have dates attached to them. A desire would be something like "visit Alaska"; a goal would be something like "arrive in Fairbanks no later than 10:00pm, September 14, 1989."

A goal is a statement of a conscious intention to produce a specific result no later than a definite time in the future. Goals are expressions of your purpose. A goal gets completed; your purpose goes on and on, through the completion of many goals.

Some people go through life without goals. Most people who don't have goals experience their lives as being frustrating and directionless. The benefits of defining goals that you like are: 1) it provides focus for your activities, 2) it allows you to take responsibility for giving yourself what you want (rather than hoping), and 3) it gives you a basis for measuring your effectiveness and your progress.

Goals are meaningless if they aren't expressions of your purpose. For example, you may have always thought you wanted a Rolls Royce more than anything else. Before you spend your life working to get a Rolls Royce, I suggest that you give very careful consideration to the question, Why? Having a Rolls Royce is an excellent goal for you if it serves your purpose, but if it doesn't then it's a waste of your time and energy at worst and an effective tool for suppressing your emotions at best. Maybe you only want the Rolls Royce because when you were nineteen years old you had very low self-esteem and you dreamed of the prestige of owning a very expensive car as the solution to your unhappiness. Maybe your desire for a Rolls Royce comes from a desire to outdo your father. Maybe some other off-purpose motivation is the origin. Achieving a goal that serves your purpose will be a satisfaction to you forever. Achieving a goal that is off-purpose will leave you with the disconcerting feeling that you should feel more satisfied than you do.

Goals are very different from wishful thinking. Once you set a goal and have picked a date for it, take full responsibility for achieving it and pursue that goal diligently. Wishful thinking involves hope. Hope exists to suppress helplessness. If you tell yourself something like, "I hope I go to Europe some day," that means you don't think you can cause it to happen, yourself, but maybe something you can't predict will cause it. Hope is a bad substitute for certainty; hope makes a very poor supper indeed.

A goal is something that you will manifest on your own initiative. A goal naturally leads to a plan of action and to action itself.

The process I suggest for setting meaningful goals starts with listing desires and then choosing among them. The chosen desires are then converted to goals.

This is not a Discovery Writing exercise. Instead I suggest being slow, deliberate and thorough when making each list.

THE GOALS PROCESS

1. Complete each list, listing the items for each list in whatever order they come to mind and in whatever wording comes to mind first. Let yourself think about what you desire without consideration of whether you could accomplish it or how you could accomplish it.

1a. Make a list of 20 desires you have for the World. For example: peace, a balanced federal budget, a Bill of Rights for animals, etc.

1b. Make a list of 20 mental, emotional, or spiritual traits that you desire to expand in yourself. Some examples are: patience, creativity, joy, etc.

1c. Make a list of 20 things you desire in your relationships and your social life. For example: more peaceful communication with my wife, more respect from my boss, more friends to play backgammon with, etc.

1d. Make a list of 20 desires for your physical body and health. For example, increased endurance, no more heartburn, healing for that pain in the knee, etc.

1e. Make a list of 20 things you would like to learn or skills you would like to develop. For example: flying an airplane, speaking French, learning about marketing, etc.

1f. Make a list of 20 desires for your business, profession, or career. For example: a personal secretary, desktop publishing capability, someone to market my music tapes, etc.

1g. Make a list of 20 accomplishments you desire. For example: becoming a Direct Distributor, winning the Nobel Prize, writing a book that sells over 100,000 copies, etc.

1h. Make a list of 20 things you desire to experience. For example: skydiving, visiting the Mayan ruins in Yucatan, living in Bangkok with a Thai girlfriend, etc.

1i. Make a list of 20 problems to which you desire solutions. For example: never having enough money left at the end of the month, gaining weight too easily, the greenhouse effect, etc.

1j. Make a list of 20 things you would like to have. For example: $50,000 in savings, a golden retriever, a house in Malibu, etc.

2. After you have listed all 200 desires, go back over all these desires and choose which ones support your purpose in life the most. I suggest choosing three. Choose *solely* on the basis of what supports

your purpose most, even if you experience emotional attachment to some of the other desires. Nothing says you will only achieve the ones you select in this process. Achieving the ones that support your purpose the most will give you the greatest sense of fulfillment and will further your life the most. Giving priority to the most purposeful goals will maximize your ability to satisfy all your other desires, too.

3. Next, convert your three chosen desires into goals. You do this by making them concrete and by setting dates for their accomplishment.

3a. Take each desire and figure out some way to make it concrete, measurable. Ask yourself, how will I know when this is completed?

"Well, now we've seen it."

For some desires this is very easy. For example, if your desire is to own a computer, it's pretty obvious when you've obtained one. It's an art to make some desires concrete, however. For example, cultivating patience might be what would serve your purpose the most. How would you know when you became more patient? One way is to figure out something that you could accomplish that would require patience. Perhaps there's a 1000-page book you've wanted to read but haven't because you lacked the patience. Or maybe you enjoy some things about fishing but don't have the patience, then going on a fishing trip and enjoying the whole thing might be your sign that you have become more patient. Another way is to decide on something you could do on a regular basis to cultivate patience and then do that every day for some set amount of time. An example might be meditating for an hour a day for 90 days in a row. The point is to do something to make the desire concrete so that you will have a definite moment when you can say to yourself, "Now I have achieved that goal."

3b. In setting dates, you want to make the date of completion soon enough to motivate you to take immediate action, but far enough away so as not to feel too overwhelmed.

To further support you in setting goals consider these characteristics of a good goal:

CHARACTERISTICS OF A GOOD GOAL
A. Supports your purpose in life
B. Challenging
C. Attainable
D. Has a definite date of completion
E. Lends itself to planning
F. Congruent with your other goals
G. Supports your enthusiasm
H. Can be stated in six words or less
I. Can be supported by other people
J. Will give you a sense of accomplishment
K. Congruent with your values
L. Supports all parts of your life
M. Will give you pleasure both while you are working toward it and when you complete it.
N. Fits the lifestyle that you prefer
O. Gives you enough leisure time

111

P. Supports you in cultivating the qualities of creativity

Q. Makes you a better person

R. Improves your health

S. Increases your wealth

T. Improves your social life

If your chosen goal doesn't fit any of those characteristics, I suggest modifying it somewhat so that it does or else selecting another goal.

The next chapter, Creative Time Management, tells how to make plans and schedules to help you with achieving your goals.

CHAPTER 9

CREATIVE TIME MANAGEMENT

This chapter tells you how to set up your own effective time management system. The system explained in this chapter is called Creative Time Management and is designed to maximize the ease with which you manifest your creativity in your life.

The purpose of time-management is to reduce overwhelm and increase certainty. I have two ways that I like to explain overwhelm:

The first is, "Overwhelm means the lack of a plan that you expect to work." When you know what you want to accomplish, the steps to accomplish that, and when and how to do each step, then you have the opposite of overwhelm — you have as much certainty as is humanly possible that you will get the result you want.

The second is, "You feel overwhelmed when you are trying to deal with too large a portion of something at one time." For instance if your goal is to write a book, thinking about the entire project may well make you feel overwhelmed. But if you just focus on the paragraph you're working on, you'll feel enthusiastic, creative and fine. You don't have to take your whole lunch in one swallow. Good time management includes breaking your projects down into "bite-sized" pieces.

THE MOST IMPORTANT THING TO KEEP IN MIND ABOUT TIME MANAGEMENT:

Managing your time well requires that you have a clear sense of your own values and a definite knowledge of your purpose in life. Otherwise, you are not fully your own person and managing your time more efficiently simply makes you a more efficient slave to the desires of others.

Therefore I strongly urge you to do all the processes in chapters 6-8 first before you set up this time management system.

WHY I CREATED THE CREATIVE TIME MANAGEMENT SYSTEM

I developed the Creative Time Management System to satisfy my own needs for planning. I'll describe my needs for a time management system. This will aid you in custom fitting the time-management system to yourself.

I am a very busy person. At this writing I am leading weekend seminars seven weekends out of every eight during a ten-month seminar season (I take December and January off). I have been leading seminars on that schedule since May of 1985 (this is April, 1989). Most weeks I fly somewhere on Thursday, lead a seminar and fly back again on Monday. This leaves basically Tuesdays and Wednesdays for handling business, writing, and giving private consultations. I must therefore manage my time very carefully.

For a time management system to work for me it must have the following characteristics:

1. It must remind of what I want and need to do.
2. It must enable me to be on time for appointments with people.
3. It must enable me to schedule time off.
4. It must allow me to schedule in all the activities that need to be done so that I can have a reasonable sense of when each thing is going to get done and a feeling of confidence that it will get done.
5. It has to be simple.
6. It has to be flexible.
7. It must be expandable.
8. It must be absolutely portable and take up very little space.
9. It must facilitate project planning.
10. It has to allow for my penchant for doing things at unusual times of day.
11. It must facilitate my setting priorities.
12. I want it to be inexpensive.
13. It has to coordinate my personal life with my business life.
14. It must enable me to put my good ideas into action.
15. I want it to it coordinate with my money management system, too.

The Creative Time Management system satisfies all of my needs perfectly and is the only time management system I have ever seen that does nearly all of that so well. It costs next to nothing because you make it yourself from inexpensive materials. You can learn to use it in just a few minutes and have it set up and working for you in about an hour. After that it takes only a few minutes a day to keep your time organized perfectly.

Your time management needs may be very similar to mine or they might be very different. You can, if you wish, use this entire system exactly as described here, use part of it, use none of it, or modify it to suit yourself. You'll probably find that it interfaces well with whatever time-management system you are presently using, so there will be essentially no trauma involved shifting over to this new system.

First I'll give you an overview of how the system works, then detailed instructions for getting started and using the System on a daily basis.

OVERVIEW OF THE CREATIVE TIME MANAGEMENT SYSTEM

Effective time management consists almost entirely of two things, setting priorities and being reminded of what to do next.

The core of the Creative Time Management System is a stack of "blank business cards" on which you write planned activities, one activity per card. These "Activity Cards" are kept categorized within the stack, separated by slightly longer, colored, "Category Cards." (The Materials Appendix tells how to get both kind of cards very inexpensively and quickly at any local printer.) The activities of immediate priority are pulled from their categories and put in order at the top of the stack. Blank cards are kept at the back so that whenever you think of something else you plan on doing you can write a new card for it.

This system is like a very advanced "to-do list." It never lets you forget to do anything, once you write it on a card. There are activities in life that one only does once and there are activities that one does repeatedly. With this system, when you have completed something that you plan on doing again, you simply put its card back in its category. When you are planning what to do with your time you simply thumb through the cards and pull the cards for the things you want to schedule.

The cards make it easy to set priorities and easy to decide what order to do things in.

The system enables you to coordinate all departments of your life together, because you keep cards for every part of your life in the same stack.

You will still need some kind of system to coordinate activities with the calendar and the clock. Depending on your needs and preferences

116

you can use either an appointment calendar purchased in a store, or the Detail Schedules I'm going to describe to you, or some combination of both. (Detail Schedules have the substantial benefit of being much more flexible than any appointment calendar could be.) Regardless of what kind of time-scheduling system you use, you'll find that the Activity Cards are invaluable in helping you plan your activities.

You can keep your cards bound together with a rubber band or similar device and easily carry them in your pocket, briefcase or purse. The complete stack of cards is only 4 inches long by two inches wide and two inches thick, at most. (My stack is never more than two inches thick and I am very busy.) The smallest cassette recorders take up more space! Additionally, you don't always have to take the entire stack with you when you go out, you can take only the priority cards, maybe an eighth of an inch thick.

HOW TO SET UP THE CREATIVE TIME MANAGEMENT SYSTEM

I suggest that you read through this entire section first and then actually follow the instructions and set up your system.

To set up this system there are certain materials that you will need to acquire. All of them are inexpensive and easy to get.

MATERIALS NEEDED:

• At least 500 business-card-size blank, white cards, for making Activity Cards.

• At least 20 slightly longer cards, of your favorite color, for making Category Cards.

Your local print shop can make these for you in one day or even while you wait (it only takes them about 5 to 10 minutes to make a huge number of them), at very low cost, using their hydraulic paper cutter. The Materials Appendix explains exactly what to order and about how much a print shop will probably charge you.

• Some rubber bands or some other way of keeping your cards together.

• Some kind of calendar — your appointment calendar if you have one.

MAKING THE ACTIVITY CARDS

Start by making Activity Cards. Write the activity on the card so that when you hold the card "vertically" you write starting at the top. Make the cards for the following types of activities:

1. All the things you can think of that are on your mind right now — the things you keep running through your mind to make sure you don't forget them. This might include phone calls you need to make, things you need to buy, things you've told people you'd do for them, etc.

2. All the mundane activities you can think of that you would want included in this system. For example, do the laundry, make an appointment for getting your teeth cleaned, get an oil change, etc.

You don't need to include things that are so habitual that you don't ever need to be reminded of them. (I don't have cards for getting out of bed or shaving, for instance.)

3. Next, take your #1 goal from the Goals Process you did in Chapter 8. Write down on cards all the steps that there are in achieving that goal. Another way to say that is all the activities you can think of that would move you toward achieving that goal. Make these steps as "bite-sized" as possible.

Repeat this process with each of the other chosen goals. You only need one card per activity, so if two goals both have one step in common, then you only need to make one card for that. (For example you may have two projects in mind that both require getting a P.O. box. You only need one card that says, "Get a P.O. Box," no matter how many different projects require that.)

4. Make cards for anything else you can think of that you might want cards for. Inevitably you'll keep adding activities as you go through life using this system; you don't need to think of everything right now.

The next step is to sort your activity cards into categories and make the Category Cards. The main purpose of this is to make it easy to find the Activity Card you are looking for when you are using the system — you can think of it as a filing system.

MAKING CATEGORY CARDS

To make the Category Cards, proceed as follows:

1. Go through your Activity cards one-by-one and put each card into a group with other cards of similar type. It is OK for one of the categories to be "Miscellaneous" but if you have many cards in that category you can probably create one or more new categories with more descriptive names.

In doing this process with several groups of people I found out that no two people categorize activities just alike. In fact, you may learn some interesting things about yourself just by categorizing your activities. After you've used this system for a while you will probably want to rearrange your categories somewhat.

2. When every card has been sorted into a group, decide on a short, memorable, descriptive name for each one of the groups. The colored cards are slightly longer than the Activity Cards so that you can read the names of the categories when all the cards are in one big stack. Write the names at the very top of the colored cards, small enough for the entire name to fit on the part of the card that sticks up above the Activity Cards. Follow this process with each one of the groups.

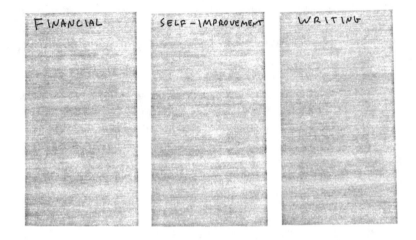

Now put all the cards together into one stack as follows:

1. Put all the Activity Cards of one category together, in front of the Category Card identifying that group. It easier to work with the cards when the Activity Cards are in front than when the Category Card is in front, covering them up.

2. Put the groups, with Category Card in back, in alphabetical order. You can put them in any order that makes sense to you; I like alphabetical order because it's easy.

3. If you want to, you can put the Activity Cards within in each category in order, somehow, too. I tend not to do that very much, simply because there aren't so many cards within each group that I feel like I need to. Some people to whom I've shown this system find it very helpful to keep the cards within each group in priority order, chronological order, etc. Sometimes I keep all the cards for a project

120

in order, sometimes not. You can experiment and see what you like best.

In the course of teaching this system to many people I found that it was helpful to tell people what categories I use, so they'd have an example. My categories as I'm sitting here:

Advertising
Anne (a business associate)
Automobile
Book
Computer
Financial
Household
I.V.C. (International Vivation Community)
Letters
Media
Office Management
Phil & Jeanne (business associates)
Phone calls
Purchases
RecreationTapes
Travel readiness
Writing

I used to have a category called "Errands" for all the things I run around doing with the car when I'm in-town (dry-cleaner, groceries, etc.), but I no longer think about it quite that way. Nowadays I just pull all the cards from their various categories and put them in the order in which I intend to do them while I'm out.

Obviously your categories are not going to be just like mine. This system is infinitely flexible and you can change the categories around whenever you want.

Additionally, you will probably want to go through and "re-categorize" your cards periodically. Categories change with time because your life changes with time and they'll also change somewhat as you become more accustomed to using the system. Sometimes you may want to make a category broader by combining several categories that are closely related (for instance you might want to put "Letters" and "Articles" into one category called "Writing") or you might want to divide one much used category into several smaller ones (for instance you might want to divide "Recreation" into "Sports," "Entertainment" and "Vacations.")

SETTING PRIORITIES

The main advantage of using cards for this system is that they make it easy to set priorities.

There are really two ways of prioritizing cards in this system — one that you'd use when using the cards alone and one that you'd use when using Detail Schedules, explained below. I suggest starting off with using the cards alone until you become familiar with using the cards. Then I suggest using Detail Schedules for a while to get a sense of whether you like using them.

In this section I shall describe how to set priorities using the cards alone. I'll explain how to prioritize when coordinating with Detail Schedules in the Detail Schedules section.

When using the cards alone you prioritize chronologically, i.e., in the order that you plan on doing the activities.

1. Make a Category Card for your priorities. I suggest calling this "Priority".

2. Now go through all the cards in your entire stack and pull out the ones that you think are likely candidates for immediate action. For right now you can think of this as anything you plan on doing in the next week.

You can hold the stack in one hand and "walk your fingers" through the cards with the other. Put the chosen cards in the very front of the stack, in front of the priority Category Card.

3. Now put the chosen cards in chronological order, so that the activity you will be doing first is in front.

With the priority group in front of all the others, and the cards in chronological order the immediate task at hand is clearly visible even when all the cards are bound together.

4. Now make a Category card called "Today". Go down through the cards in front and put the "Today" card behind the last one you intend to get done today or by the end of tomorrow.

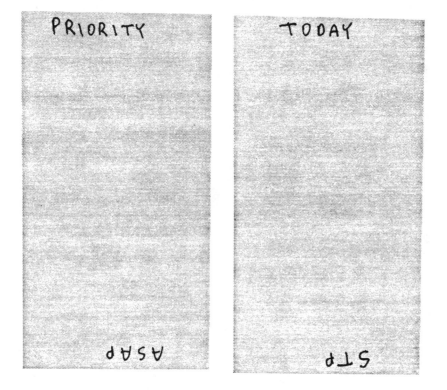

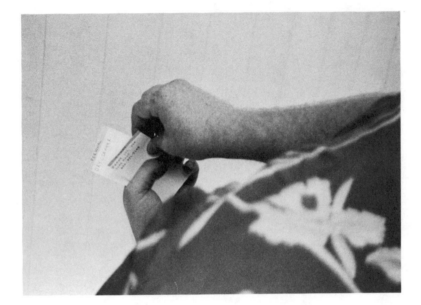

HOW TO USE THE CREATIVE TIME-MANAGEMENT CARDS ON A DAILY BASIS

Using the cards-alone system on a daily basis requires only ten to fifteen minutes a day to greatly increase your productivity and organization. You can plan your activities either in the morning or on the night before (or any other way you like). Simply hold the deck of cards in one hand and "walk your fingers" through them with the other. Pull the cards for your priority activities, add new cards as needed, put all the priority cards in chronological order and put the Today card behind that last one you plan to accomplish today.

As you complete each task put the card back in its category if you want to be reminded to do it again, or discard it if you only needed to do that activity once. (I bend such cards in half to make sure I know to not put them back in.)

Activities you plan to get done today but don't actually get done, are still in the stack for you the next day.

Carry the cards with you and whenever you have a good idea (probably several times each day if you're like me) just jot it down on a card and put it in your system. Your good ideas will never go to waste again!

HELPFUL HINTS FOR USING CREATIVE TIME MANAGEMENT CARDS

This system interfaces very elegantly with Discovery Writing. For example, if you are interested in increasing your income, then I urge you to take the 2 to 3 minutes daily to write a Discovery List of ways to increase your income (Chapter 4). Some of the ideas you get will inspire your enthusiasm and you can make Activity Cards for these and put them into your system.

I usually share office space with two or three co-workers, including my secretary. All of us use the Creative Time Management system. Each of us has Category Cards of a different color, I use blue. By using different colors we can distinguish our own cards from each others' at a glance.

When we want to suggest activities for each other, we simply write them on cards and either hand them to each other or put them in each others' in-boxes. It's a lovely feeling to pull cards from my system and give them to my secretary to do! This is a very convenient system for delegating activities and for supplementing other forms of intra-office communication.

You can easily update your card system and/or your Detail Schedules while waiting for your food to come at a restaurant, while waiting for the bus etc.

Periodically go through all your cards with the thought in mind: "Do I really need this card?" and remove all the ones that duplicate or that you really don't need.

If you're like anybody else whom I've taught this system, you're probably starting to grasp already how much this will increase your productivity, your creativity and your peace of mind! You may not need anything else at all for managing your time perfectly than just the Creative Time Management cards and a calendar for keeping track of meetings with other people. Appointment calendars have their limitations, however, and depending on your time management needs, you may want to use a superior method of scheduling, which is described in the next system.

DETAIL SCHEDULES

With any time-management system, you have to coordinate your activities with both the calendar and the clock. Most time-management systems are not flexible enough to really allow you to do that very well. Because of their inflexibility, the calendars that most people use are really only good for scheduling appointments with other people. If you were taking your car and going on errands with visits to six stores, you would almost certainly not put anticipated times of arrival at each store in your appointment calendar. It is very helpful to have a system that allows you to make time projections of that type, however. Real mastery over time requires it. Without it, you'll probably plan more things than you can get done and feel overwhelmed because you never really know when things are going to get done.

Detail Schedules give you the kind of flexibility that allows you really to plan when to do what.

Sometimes things take longer than expected. When that happens, either the times of everything after that need to be pushed back or one of the later activities needs to be eliminated and rescheduled for another day. Detail Schedules make this type of adjustment easy.

Sometimes you'll think of something else you can do on the same errand or while waiting. Sometimes you may get called by someone who tells you he or she will be late for an appointment with you so you'll want to plan something else to do during that time. Sometimes you'll simply remember an additional step in getting something done. In these cases you'll want to write another activity in between two that are already scheduled. Detail Schedules allow for this type of flexible scheduling of activities.

You can purchase Detail Schedules inexpensively ready-made (see the Materials Appendix).

DETAIL SCHEDULE FOR

TIME			ACCOMPLISH

Each page of the Detail Schedule is divided by horizontal lines into ten main sections, one for each activity to be scheduled. At the top right of each page is written the date that is being scheduled. You can use more than one page per date, whenever you have more than ten activities to schedule per day.

The page is divided vertically into to two main sections, one for writing in a time and one for writing in an activity.

The time section is divided into three columns. This is to allow the time that an activity is scheduled to be changed, if need be, during the course of the day.

DETAIL SCHEDULE FOR TU 19 MAY

TIME			ACCOMPLISH
8:00			GO JOGGING WITH RALPH
9:30			PHONE CALLS
11:00			WORK ON BOOK
2:00			GO TO POST OFFICE
3:00			MEET MARY AT MY OFFICE
4:30			GO HOME. MAKE DINNER.
7:30			BE AT UNITY CHURCH TO LEAD SEMINAR
9:00			MEET WITH REV. BURNES

Each main section of the activity column is divided horizontally into three lines. This is so you can interpolate activities between ones originally scheduled. For example, suppose you have had it scheduled to go to the post office at 2pm and then meet Mary at your office at 3pm. You might get a message to phone George and want to schedule phoning him after you get back from the post office but before Mary is due to arrive, say at 2:40. You would simply write "Phone George" either on the line right above "Meet Mary" or on the line right below "Go to post office".

2:00			GO TO POST OFFICE
3:00			MEET MARY AT MY OFFICE

2:00			GO TO POST OFFICE
2:40			PHONE GEORGE
3:00			MEET MARY AT MY OFFICE

There are three time columns and three activity lines per main section simply because in the course of using the Detail Schedule I discovered that I often needed more than two spaces for changes but I almost never needed more than three.

130

The Detail Schedule pages are kept in a three-ring binder. Blank Detail Schedules are kept at the back.best.

In the inside of the front cover of the notebook there is a calendar for the year.

You don't have to keep a sheet for every day of the year. Simply keep a sheet for the dates that you have something scheduled. Whenever you schedule something for a certain date, simply leaf through the Detail Schedules until you come to the schedule for that date, or the dates before or after that date. If there is not already a page for that date, you simply write that date on the top right of a blank Detail Schedule, insert it in its proper place and write the scheduled item into one of the activity blocks.

Always write the activity on the middle line of the activity block. Always write the time in the left column of the time section. You can choose which block to write the activity in according to your own judgment about how many activities you will ultimately plan before and after the item you are scheduling. You don't need to put the activity in the "right block" for this to work.

You will probably often have more than one page per day. For a given day in the future you start off having no pages for that day. Then, the first time you plan something for that day you make a page for it and put one item on that page. As the day draws closer, you plan it in more detail, first filling the sheet, then, perhaps creating one or two other pages for that day.

When the day is past, you can discard the used Detail Schedules for that day, but first look over the Detail Schedules to see if you can learn anything about yourself in relationship to time and planning. One of the advantages of using Detail Schedules is that if you habitually underestimate the time it takes to accomplish something, you will find that out and be able to make corrections.

DETAIL SCHEDULE FOR TU 19 MAY

	TIME		ACCOMPLISH
8:00			GO JOGGING WITH RALPH
9:00			GROCERY STORE
9:30	9:45		PHONE CALLS
11:00			WORK ON BOOK
1:00			LUNCH
2:00			GO TO POST OFFICE
2:40			PHONE GEORGE
3:00			MEET MARY AT MY OFFICE
4:30			GO HOME. MAKE DINNER.
7:30			BE AT UNITY CHURCH TO LEAD SEMINAR
9:00			SEE IF JULIE IS FREE
9:00			MEET WITH REV. BURNES

Of course also reschedule anything you planned but didn't accomplish, before discarding the Detail Schedule at the end of the day.

When you are using Detail Schedules, you prioritize the Activity Cards differently than when you are using just the cards. Instead of putting the priority cards in chronological order you put them in order of importance.

For example, if you look at all the Activity Cards in your stack, there will be one single most important thing for you to do. This may not be the thing you would do first, however. There may be preliminary steps. Or maybe you have to wait for the bank to open on Monday or something. The most important thing might even be months away!

Pick the best time for getting that most important thing done and put it in your Detail Schedule for that time. Then pick the best time for getting the second most important thing done. Following this procedure will create your ideal plan.

What actually happens will be different from your plan, but the Detail Schedule is flexible enough to allow for this. By having a plan you can be as sure as is humanly possible that you will accomplish what you set out to do.

Since you prioritize differently when using the Detail Schedule than when using the cards alone, you might choose different names for the priority categories. When I'm using Detail Schedules I have mildly humorous names for my two categories of priority. Instead of calling the more immediate category Today and the less immediate category Priority, I call the lesser of the two priorities ASAP (for "As soon as possible") and the greater of the two priorities STP (for "Sooner than possible"). You can call them whatever you like, obviously.

HELPFUL HINTS FOR USING DETAIL SCHEDULES

Schedule time off first. Be honest about when you will work and when you won't. Give yourself adequate time off. Don't become a burned out workaholic or you'll wind up accomplishing less, not more.

There are different kinds of time off, each of which may be important to you: Time off alone, time off with your mate (or for dating), time off with friends of the same sex as you, time off for intellectual pursuits, time off for physical activities, time off in nature, time off for cultural activities, time off for housework, etc.

Keep your time off clearly separated from your work time. By planning well you can get more done and have more time off, too.

Be sure to put all your appointments in the Detail Schedule. Keep your social events and business events in the same system — a dual scheduling system will make you go nuts because you'll double-book sometimes.

When you first start using the Detail Schedules you may experience frustration at how different your planning is from what you actually do. This is normal and good, although it may not feel good while it's going on. This is a process of learning about yourself. If you go through life telling yourself you ought to get more done every day than you really can get done, that same frustration is there anyway — using the Detail Schedules will simply activate the frustration and actually do something to heal it. Don't turn the Detail Schedules into a club for beating yourself up, though.

If it gets too activating, learn what you can and give yourself a break from it for a while. When you take it up again loosen up your schedule and lighten up your expectations. These can be wonderful tools for helping chronic Type A (stress-creating) individuals learn to be more reasonable.

If you aren't busy enough (or ambitious enough) to need Detail Schedules, then don't use them!

You goals, your activity cards and your money management system all coordinate together into one easy-to-use system.

HABITS AND PRACTICES

People are largely creatures of habit. Bad habits can rob you of energy, money and time. Good habits require cultivation. The term I use for a good habit that is under cultivation is a "practice."

It is important that you make it a practice to use your time management system every day. If you use it only rarely it will rarely give you much benefit. If you are using the cards alone, then be sure to go through them every day and re-prioritize them according to what you have accomplished and according to the good ideas you have had.

If you use Detail Schedules, make sure that you plan each day thoroughly either in the morning or on the night before.

You'll probably find that if you have set practices that you go through every morning and every night that you will get more from your time each day.

Cultivate a sense of daily and weekly rhythm. There is much power in having your life become variations on themes. By doing the same kind of things over and over, mastery can be attained.

An excellent idea is to plan out what an ideal day would be like for you. How would you like your ideal day to begin? What would you like to do and experience during your ideal day? What would you eat on your ideal day? How would you like your ideal day to end? Do this same thing with your ideal week. Do what you can to make your days and your weeks as much like your ideal day and ideal week as possible.

Develop practices of doing daily self-improvement. Don't let bad habits get a foothold. The first step in eliminating any bad habit is telling the truth about it. Be patient with yourself but work diligently to cultivate practices that serve you and to eliminate habits that don't serve you.

A good method for staying on track with your practices is making checklists of things you want to be reminded to do. Simply list the items on paper with a place for checking them off in the left margin. You can use these for an incredible variety of practices. Some examples are: a packing checklist to make sure you get everything you need when you're going on a trip, a checklist of practices to engage in on a daily basis, a checklist of things for an employee to do once a day, once a week, or once a month, etc. When you have a checklist you like you can get it photocopied and padded.

An even better method, if you have personal computer, is to keep the checklists in a file in the word processor and print a fresh one each time — this allows you to make changes easily.

Your time is your most valuable asset — it is the stuff life is made of. Managing your time well will enable you to have all of your fondest desires satisfied.

CHAPTER 10

CREATIVE MONEY MANAGEMENT

As I'm sure you've learned by now, creativity can be well applied to every aspect of life. The solution to every problem and the quickest route to success in any venture come from creativity.

This is particularly true with regards to money and business. Creativity applied to the financial arena of a person's life can do much: it can increase income, it can handle bad habits, it can break negative family patterns regarding money, it can help a person find a more fulfilling career, it can greatly help a person increase sales or succeed in a business venture, it can even add zest to mundane activities like paying bills.

In this chapter I present numerous ideas for how to apply creativity to money management. The ideas presented here are not even 1% of the possible applications. Use the ideas in this chapter as you wish; expect to need to modify them to fit your own situation. Perhaps more important, let these ideas provide starting places for your own creative thinking about money.

"It's mighty good eating for the pennies it costs."

Drawing by Koren; © 1973 The New Yorker Magazine, Inc.

Money management is a very broad topic, broad enough for many books; in this single chapter I am obviously not going to cover it completely. My intention is to add some ideas and processes that I believe will be helpful to a wide range of people and which I believe are not available elsewhere in the literature on money management. My favorite basic, enlightened text on prosperity is *Money is My Friend*, by Phil Laut (Vivation Publishing Co., Cincinnati, Ohio.)

The financial sphere of a person's life comprises two main endeavors: 1. making money in the first place and 2. deciding how best to utilize the money once you've succeeded in obtaining some of it.

In the absence of applying creativity to making money a person is pretty much stuck with taking whatever opportunities come along in life, with necessity generally dominating over satisfaction.

Anyone fortunate enough to develop a career that is truly fulfilling has had to apply substantial creativity many times along the way. Without creativity you will always have to be fitted to the Procrustean bed of someone else's purpose for you.

Obviously not all creative projects involve business. However, any substantial creative project requires working within a budget. Even if the project is small enough not to require much money for itself, it is still helpful not to feel overwhelmed by financial worries. While it is true that a person can be creative even in the midst of poverty or fear of poverty, one can easily see that it is not the most desirable milieu for creative endeavor.

SOME COMMENTS ON MAKING MONEY CREATIVELY

Earlier chapters in this book are readily applicable to making money and increasing income. Knowing your values and your purpose in life make it much, much easier to select a career. Discovery Writing makes it possible to figure out how to increase your income. When you have an investment goal or an earning goal, the chapter, "How to Use Discovery Writing to Achieve any Goal" will help you do your very best to attain that. Creative Time Management makes it much easier to manage your affairs well in whatever field of endeavor you choose.

Without a doubt creativity finds greater avenues of expression in self-employment than in working for someone else. This, in turn, leads to greater opportunity for increasing income and to greater creative fulfillment in general.

It is my belief that the majority of people overestimate the difficulty of self-employment and underestimate its rewards. I think many people who work at jobs would be better off being self-employed.

When you work for someone else what you are really doing is paying someone to tell you what to do. I realize this is not how most people think about it so I'll be glad to explain what I mean.

Obviously the company you work for has to make a profit on your work. If they ever come to believe that they are not making a profit on your work they will discharge you at once. If they make a profit on your work that means that you are producing more wealth than they are paying you; this is just two ways of saying the same thing. The difference between the wealth you create and what they pay you is, in reality, the amount that you are paying them to employ you. In other words, if you owned the company you would get to keep all the wealth you create instead of just part of it. If you can tell yourself what to do then you don't have to pay someone else to do so.

Another way to describe the difference between being employed by someone else and being self-employed is that when you are self-employed you sell your product or service to many customers whereas when you are employed you sell 100% of your services to your employer.

A common misconception is that there is more security in being employed than in being self-employed. If you work at a job, the amount you are paid, and whether you continue being employed there at all, are up to other people's decisions. People get laid off from jobs all the time and most people would like to be paid more by their employers. On the other hand, once you know how to make your living self-employed you can always make a living and your pay increases are up to you. All you have to do is figure out a way to increase your productivity or reduce your expenses and PRESTO! instant raise. Knowing how to make a living self-employed is the ultimate in financial security.

Virtually any form of self-employment requires selling. Selling is where the money actually comes in to any business. It is only the slightest exaggeration to say that if you can sell you can make it in self-employment and if you can't sell you can't make it until you learn to sell. Insufficient sales is by far the biggest cause of small business failure. In many types of small business your ability to sell will make a bigger difference in how much money you make than the quality of your product or service will.

This required selling scares many people away from self-employment unnecessarily. Anybody can learn how to sell effectively. It is not difficult to learn how to sell. It is even fun and the benefits you get from learning it will extend far beyond the financial realm to all aspects of your personal relationships — selling is the ultimate communication workshop.

It is true that to learn how to sell you will need both persistence and courage. It is also true that to accomplish anything of a creative nature you will need both persistence and courage anyway.

Here's how to learn how to sell:

1. Identify some item that you already know about and like, that is small enough to carry with you and that sells for between $5 and $10 retail.

2. Obtain a small quantity of this item at the wholesale price.

3. Carry one with you most everywhere you go.

4. Tell people about the product frequently and give them an opportunity to purchase one from you.

That's really all there is to it. Keep doing that until you are confident that you can sell well. It won't take long at all. Once you learn how to sell one product you will be able to sell, with only slight modification, any product or service. From then on you will always be able to make a living, in any economic circumstances.

There are many excellent books on selling, as well as seminars, cassette and video tapes, etc. My favorite book on selling is *How to Master the Art of Selling*, by Tom Hopkins (Warner Books).

Reading books, taking seminars, and so on will not teach you how to sell. Only selling will teach you that. These books and other learning aids can help you to hone your skills if you *are* selling, however. It is the kind of thing that know matter how good you are at it you can always get even better.

Don't wait for anything. I urge you to learn how to sell immediately. I think being able to sell is a fundamental, essential skill of living in modern society, similar to reading, typing, etc. I believe that teaching selling skills to everyone in the sixth grade would do more to eliminate unemployment and improve the economy than anything else could.

You don't have to quit your job to get started being self-employed. All you need are a product or service you are excited about, the means to deliver this product or service to a customer, a price that makes you a profit, and a customer. With that you are self-employed.

There are undoubtedly infinitely many ways to apply creativity to working at jobs, too.

The main point is to open your mind to finding ways to apply creativity to your career and your fund-raising efforts. Consider things you've never considered before and insist on having breakthroughs.

MANAGING YOUR MONEY CREATIVELY

Money management lends itself very well to creativity. You can create projects of various kinds to increase your mastery over the various aspects of money management. In this chapter I present numerous suggestions for creative ways to decide how best to channel money and how best to track what happens with your money, and some other ideas, as well. Naturally enough I call it "Creative Money Management."

The single most important thing in managing money is to have some method for managing it consciously. Simplicity is valuable in this, as in most things, because simplicity allows you to concentrate your mind on the problem at hand and nothing else. The simplest system that works to apply consciousness adequately is the best.

OVERVIEW OF THE CREATIVE MONEY MANAGEMENT SYSTEM

The Creative Money Management System consists of three main parts, which can be used separately or all together.

The first part is a Percentage Budget, which is not a new idea, but which I present with some new details that I think are helpful.

The second part consists of keeping charts and graphs to in order to have a broad, linear, overview of what is happening with your money.

The third part consists of creatively designed Money Projects.

Throughout this explanation I will be using the term "money structure" to mean any kind of plan or setup that you put in place to help you with managing your money.

PERCENTAGE BUDGET

A Percentage Budget is a very simple money structure in which, whenever income comes in, you divide the money among a variety of uses according to a pre-selected formula.

Here's how to set up a Percentage Budget:

1. Make a list of all the things you have been putting money into. For instance:

Rent
Mortgage
Savings
Food
Utilities
Telephone
Entertainment
Tithing
Books
Pocket money
Self-improvement seminars
Travel expense
Advertising
Inventory
Supplies
Employee expense
Taxes
Professional expense
and so on.

2. Figure out how much you have been putting into each of these, on average, per month. Use receipts, check stubs, records, memory, intuition or whatever you need to figure this out.

3. Figure out what your usual monthly income is. Most people who are employed by someone else do best to use the net income (after payroll deductions). Most people who have their own businesses do best to use the gross income (total sales).

4. Divide each of the figures you got in step 2 by the figure you got in step 3. This tells you approximately what percentage you have been allocating to each item.

5. This is very important. Look carefully at the figures you got from step 4 and decide how you would like for that to be different in the future than it has been in the past. You can change your patterns of spending by using the Percentage Budget. In time you can even make truly radical changes to your spending patterns. For now, consider making the adjustments relatively minor.

Consider saving more each month. Here are some thoughts about saving:

Most people don't save enough. Everyone needs to have at least two savings accounts, one for investments and one for large purchases.

The way to think about your Investment Savings account is that you never take money out to spend it on expenses, you only take it out to invest it in something else that gives you a higher return.

The point of this savings structure is to achieve financial independence so that you never have to work to make your living anymore. In other words, the idea is to accumulate enough capital to make your entire living off interest and dividends without having to touch the principle. This may take a while to achieve but it is definitely the right goal to have.

The way to think about your large purchases savings account is that you save money to spend on things that cost more than the amount of money you are accustomed to receiving at one time. To purchase things that cost more than you are accustomed to receiving at one time you need to either save money or go into debt (or some combination). By saving you are able to avoid the disadvantages of going into debt.

Having given careful thought to how much money you want to allocate to each of your categories, now assign a percentage to each one. Whenever money comes in you will put the assigned percentage of your income into each of the categories. Since you will be using a calculator to divide up the money (presumably) these do not need to be round numbers. As long as all the percentages add up to 100% any percentages you pick will be fine.

6. Now decide what you will actually do with the money that you allocate to each of the categories. For example, if you pay the rent monthly and you receive some money every day, where do you put the money while it is accumulating? It will be appropriate to do different things with the money for different items. Here are five possibilities that you can consider for each of your categories:

a. It might go into your pocket in cash if it is pocket money.

b. It might get mailed directly to its ultimate recipient if the amount of the payment doesn't make any difference. This is true of tithing or giving to a charity, for example.

c. It might go into its own separate bank account. Investment savings would simply be transferred into your investment savings account, for instance.

d. It might go, in cash, into an envelope in your desk. This is a good thing to do with money you spend as cash when you will never be accumulating very much of it at a time. This might be best for grocery money for instance.

e. It might go into a bank account with other funds, in which case you keep a journal that tells you how much of what is in the account has been assigned to what purpose.

7. Finally, decide how often you will re-evaluate your percentages. If you do this too frequently, it will be a nuisance and be too flexible to give you the kind of structure that will be helpful.

If you do it too infrequently, on the other hand, it won't be flexible enough to work well; for instance you might end up accumulating far more money in one of the categories than you need to. For most people, I suggest re-doing the percentages either every two weeks or once a month.

You now have your Percentage Budget all set up! Simple, huh?

Here are some helpful hints for making this work for you:

1. Make sure you follow whatever rules you set up — don't refigure the percentages in response to impulse, or even dire necessity. Wait until it's time to do it.

2. Don't "borrow" money from one account to another. This is the Voice of Experience talking: it will look innocent and natural to do it sometimes and if you get started doing it you will inevitably blow the whole money structure out.

3. You very well might find it helpful to have a category called "Miscellaneous" that is for increasing the flexibility of the system. You put some small percentage of your income into this account and you can take it out and put it into any of the other accounts in response to either necessity or convenience. This works as a buffer to keep you from either going nuts or blowing out your structure.

4. One kind of account you might find helpful is one that has this rule, you put some percentage of your income in and on any given day you can only take out some pre-selected maximum percentage of what was in there at the start of that day. For example, I have found it helpful at times to have an account called "Business Savings" that is for business projects of various kinds with the rule that 20% of my income goes in and on no single day can I take out more than 50% of what's in there. This guarantees always having some money to apply to business opportunities that come up. I call this kind of structure "an account with a rule."

5. Put all your income initially into one bank account. This makes accounting easier.

6. If you use a system that involves transferring money from one bank account to another be sure to document these movements of money so that the I.R.S. won't think it's new income being deposited each time. If you aren't sure what it will take to make that obvious to the I.R.S., do consult an accountant (or maybe your banker) about it.

7. You can coordinate a "purchases" account with your Creative Time Management system by keeping the Activity Cards in your Purchases Category in priority order. Whenever enough money accumulates in your purchases account, spend it on the front card in the Purchases Category. This same type of coordination between the time and money systems will work with other kind of projects as well.

USING CHARTS AND GRAPHS IN MONEY MANAGEMENT

One of the things a good money management system does for its user is give a long-term sense of what is happening with his or her money. For this purpose, charts and graphs can show what has been happening very clearly. If you are self-employed, even partially, charts and graphs are indispensable.

In this book, when I say "chart" I mean statistics represented as numerals in some format resembling a spread sheet or a columnar pad. When I say "graph" I mean a visually meaningful symbolic representation of statistical information. I usually like to use both a chart and a graph for most statistics in my business and my personal finance. The numeric values used in a chart are more precise, more flexible and make graphing easier. My mind can grasp the essence of what's been happening far better from a graph, however.

In this chapter I shall make reference to self-improvement techniques that are described in detail in other chapters of this book. For more information about "Discovery Writing" see Chapter 4. For more information about "Vivation" see Chapters 11 through 13. For more information about "Affirmations" see Chapters 11 and 14.

When you are doing any kind of self-improvement project regarding money or prosperity consciousness, I strongly urge you to keep charts and graphs to see if what you are doing is working. Money, by its very nature, lends itself extremely well to objective measurement. Especially when you are working with prosperity Affirmations, measure your results objectively. Affirmations can be extremely useful when used well, but they have no built-in mechanism to prevent you from simply deluding yourself. (Vivation, however, does have such a built-in mechanism — a major benefit of the process.) My observation is that a whole lot of people increase their self-delusion about money by using prosperity Affirmations poorly. By keeping charts and graphs you can prevent that from happening. Please heed this warning.

The keeping of charts and graphs also works well as a self-improvement technique on its own. You'll naturally find yourself modifying your behavior in order to make the graphs come out looking better. A simple example is that if you just carry a pocket notebook with you and write down everything you spend money on, you'll spend less money. The same thing works for all other aspects of keeping track of your monetary results.

Charts and graphs can be kept in a notebook or in a computer. I have a very fine computer, but I don't keep my charts and graphs in it because I find it just as easy, and far more portable, to keep them on paper in a notebook.

For making charts you can simply use ruled notebook paper and make your own columns or you can use the columnar pads that are made for this purpose. For graphs, you will want graph paper, obviously.

THINGS YOU CAN GRAPH

This is a list of some of the things you might find it helpful to graph:

You can graph your income.

You can graph your net worth.

You can graph the value of your investments.

You can graph your total money.

You can graph the amount that is in an account with a rule.

You can graph the income you make on some particular thing.

You can graph expenses.

You can graph your progress toward a goal.

You can keep a chart of how many days you have stuck to your money structure.

You can graph how much time (or how many times) you do something intended to improve your financial situation. For example you can keep a chart of the number of sales calls you make each day or the amount of time you spend on Affirmation Discovery each day.

You can graph the percentage of your money that goes to each type of expense.

If you have income from a variety of sources you can graph the percentage of your income that comes from each source.

You can also graph anything else that is quantifiable!

CHARTS ARE SIMPLE

Simply have the left-hand column be for the date and other columns of whatever you are keeping track of.

It's OK to keep a chart without using a graph but I don't recommend keeping track of something on a graph only without using a chart. The graph is too approximate and if you decide later that you want a different kind of graph you'll find it much easier to create it from a chart than from another graph.

TYPES OF GRAPHS

For something that fluctuates up and down within a period of time, (the value of your investments, for example) you can use a "high, low, close graph."

For something that only has a total per period of time (income for example) you can use a bar graph.

For measuring progress toward a goal, you can use a progress projection graph.

For something you intend to minimize you can use an inverted bar graph.

For graphing percentages and amount simultaneously you can use a sectioned bar graph (for example if you have income from several sources and you want to show both the total income and the amount from each source).

INSTRUCTIONS FOR MAKING GRAPHS:
HIGH, LOW, CLOSE GRAPH OF NET WORTH:

Keep a daily chart with at least all of the following columns: date, total assets, total debt, total bills due, and net worth; once a week put the statistics on a graph.

DAILY CHART OF NET = CASH − (DEBTS + BILLS)

DATE	DESCRIPTION	CASH			DEBT + BILLS			NET		
		IN	OUT	BALANCE	UP	DOWN	BALANCE	HIGH	LOW	FINAL
APR 25	START			9331			3912			5419
25	PRIV. SESSIONS	360		9691			3912	5779		
25	EXPENSE		56	9635			3912	5779	5419	5723
APR 26	PRIV. SESSIONS	360		9995			3912			
26	SEMINAR ENR.	390		10,385			3912	6473		
26	EXPENSE		91	10,294			3912	6473	5723	6382
APR 27	SEMINAR ENR.	195		10,489			3912	6577		
27	EXPENSE		144	10,345			3912	6577	6382	6433
APR 28	SEMINAR ENR.	390		10,735			3912	6823		
28	EXPENSE		205	10,530			3912	6823	6433	6618
APR 29	PHONE BILL			10,530	319		4231		6299	
29	PHONE BILL		319	10,211		319	3912			
29	PRIV. SESSIONS	240		10,451			3912			
29	EXPENSE		31	10,420			3912	6618	6299	6508
APR 30	PRIV. SESSIONS	300		10,720			3912			
30	SEMINAR ENR.	585		11,305			3912	7393		
30	PMT. TO R. LUOKE		500	10,805		500	3412			
30	EXPENSE		44	10,761			3412	7393	6508	7349
MAY 1	RENT		700	10,061			3412		6649	
1	PMT ON VISA		128	9933		128	3284			
1	PMT ON MC		75	9858		75	3209			
1	PRIV. SESSIONS	360		10,218			3209			
1	EXPENSE		89	10,129			3209	7349	6649	6920
MAY 2	UTILITY BILL			10,129	191		3400		6729	
2	PRIV. SESSIONS	240		10,369			3400			
2	SEMINAR ENR.	390		10,759			3400	7359		
2	EXPENSE		66	10,693			3400	7359	6729	7293
MAY 3	PRIV. SESSIONS	300		10,993			3400			
3	SEMINAR ENR.	195		11,188			3400	7788		
3	EXPENSE		41	11,147			3400	7788	7293	7747
MAY 4	PRIV. SESSIONS	285		11,432			3400	8032		
4	EXPENSE		50	11,382			3400	8032	7747	7982

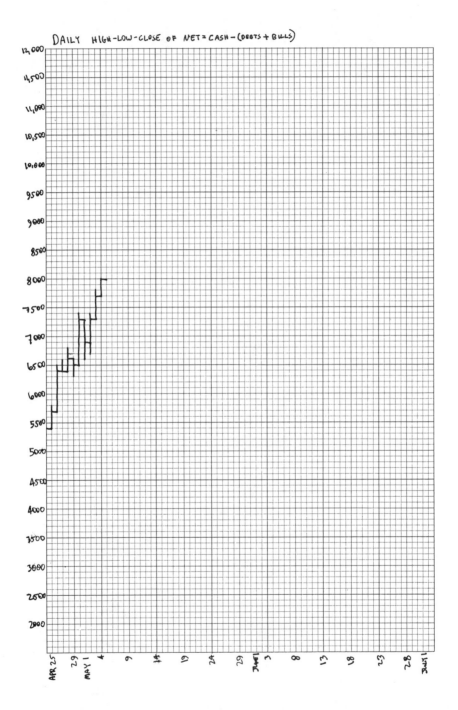

DAILY HIGH-LOW-CLOSE OF NET = CASH - (DEBTS + BILLS)

In the total assets column put the total of all your bank accounts and all your cash, the value of your stock portfolio or equity in real estate measured by some consistent system, and if you have a good accounting system for accounts receivable you can add that in, too.

Total debt is what you use for the total of all your credit cards, loans, etc.

Total bills means the total of everything you owe on regular expenses: your phone bill, your gas bill, etc. You can either put your rent in this system as something that accumulates throughout the month, or just put all of it in on the day its due; using the same system consistently is more important than which system you use.

Add your total debt and your total bills together and subtract that from your total assets, to get your net worth.

Once a week make a vertical line with its high end at the highest your net worth was during the week and its low end at the lowest your net worth was during the week and a one-column horizontal mark where it was at the end of the week.

At the bottom of the first vertical column write the date of the end of the first one-week period. Four columns later write the date of the end of the fifth week and then write in the date every five weeks thereafter. On the horizontal line headers at the left margin, put amounts of money. Here's how to figure out the amounts:

1. Figure out what increment each horizontal line is worth. You will want the length of your weekly vertical lines to be between three and ten horizontal lines long most of the time.

2. Figure out your current net worth and round that to the nearest round number in the increments your figured out in step 1. Put that round number 30 squares up from the bottom of the page. Note that the nature of net worth is that it might be below zero or it might be above zero. You may have a zero line somewhere on your chart or the whole chart might be above zero or below zero.

3. Mark every 5th line up and down from the starting point.

BAR GRAPH OF INCOME

There are various ways of thinking about income: if you have a job, you can think in terms of your gross income before deductions or your net income after deductions. If you have your own business you can think in terms of your gross sales before subtracting expenses or in terms of your net profit after subtracting expenses. For most people with jobs it is probably more meaningful to track the net. For most self-employed people it is probably more meaningful (and simpler by far) to track the gross.

CHART OF DAILY INCOME

DATE	FROM	FOR	FORM	AMOUNT
APRIL 25	C. ENTE	PRIV. SESS.	CHECK	$180.00
"	D. FORACRE	PRIV. SESS.	CHECK	180.00
APRIL 26	G. MCINTYRE	PRIV. SESS.	CHECK	180.00
"	L. PALOU	PRIV. SESS.	CHECK	180.00
"	L. PALOU	SEM. ENR.	CHECK	195.00
"	G. LORENZA	SEM. ENR.	M.C.	195.00
APRIL 27	M. BALANCE	SEM. ENR.	VISA	195.00
APRIL 28	K. GARVEY	SEM. ENR.	VISA	195.00
"	M. GOAN	SEM. ENR.	M.C.	195.00
APRIL 29	H. JONES	PRIV. SESS.	CHECK	180.00
"	L. HOCH	PRIV. SESS.	CASH	60.00
APRIL 30	G. CONSTANZA	PRIV. SESS.	CASH	180.00
"	L. MYERS	PRIV. SESS.	CHECK	120.00
"	L. MYERS	2 SEM. ENR.	MC	390.00
"	G. PACKER	SEM. ENR.	CHECK	195.00
MAY 1	N. GRAVES	PRIV. SESS.	CHECK	180.00
"	B. WOOD	PRIV. SESS.	CASH	180.00
MAY 2	C. ENTE	PRIV. SESS	CHECK	120.00
"	D. FORACRE	PRIV. SESS	CHECK	120.00
"	D. FORACRE	SEM. ENR.	CHECK	195.00
"	P. SAINT	SEM. ENR.	MC	195.00
MAY 3	G. MCINTYRE	PRIV. SESS	CASH	120.00
"	L. MACKIE	PRIV. SESS.	CASH	180.00
"	L. MACKIE	SEM. ENR.	VISA	195.00
MAY 4	H. LANE	PRIV. SESS.	CHECK	180.00
"	H. JONES	PRIV. SESS.	CHECK	105.00

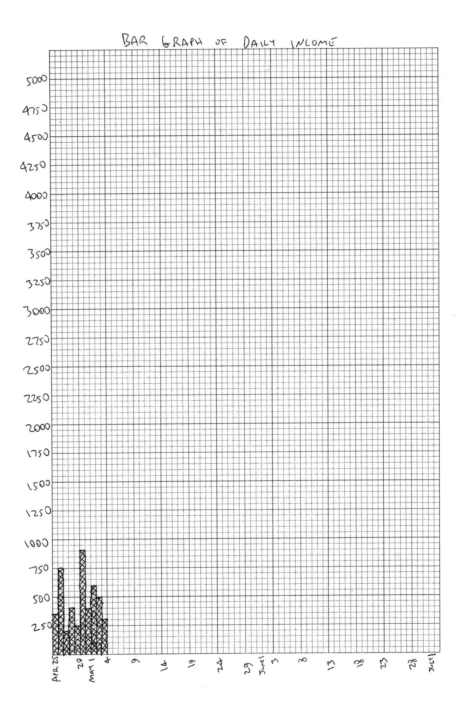

You can graph your daily, weekly or monthly income, whatever will suit your purposes best. Write the dates in at the bottom margin.

Pick a meaningful unit of money and start the vertical scale of the graph at zero at the bottom.

Simply make a bar (you can make it filled-in solid or made of x's, as you wish) that goes from the bottom to the height that represents you income for that time period.

DAILY CHART OF EXPENDITURES

DATE	TO WHOM	FOR	HOW PAID	AMOUNT
APRIL 25		MISCELLANEOUS	CASH	$56.00
APRIL 26		MISCELLANEOUS	CASH	91.00
APRIL 27		MISCELLANEOUS	CASH	144.00
APRIL 28		MISCELLANEOUS	CASH	205.00
APRIL 29	SOUTHERN BELL	PHONE BILL	CHECK	319.00
"		MISCELLANEOUS	CASH	31.00
APRIL 30	R. LUBKE	FINAL PAYMENT	CHECK	500.00
"		MISCELLANEOUS	CASH	44.00
MAY 1	B. THOMAS	RENT	CHECK	700.00
"	CITICORP	VISA PAYMENT	CHECK	128.00
"	CITIZENS	MC PAYMENT	CHECK	75.00
"		MISCELLANEOUS	CASH	89.00
MAY 2		MISCELLANEOUS	CASH	66.00
MAY 3		MISCELLANEOUS	CASH	41.00
MAY 4		MISCELLANEOUS	CASH	50.00

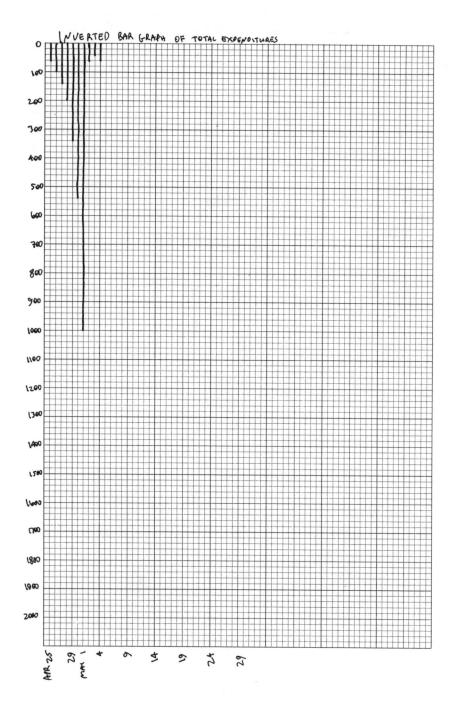

This is much like the bar graph of income except that you make the top line equal to zero and extend the line down to the level of expense for the time period.

SECTIONED, BAR GRAPH OF INCOME FROM VARIOUS SOURCES.

This is just like the bar graph of income except for one thing: you use different symbols or different colors within each bar to indicate how much of the total income came from each of various sources. You will probably want to make each horizontal line be worth a smaller increment with this chart, so that you can show more detail. Always put the various types of income on the chart in the same order and you will easily be able to see how each component of expense varies from time-period to time-period, as well as the total.

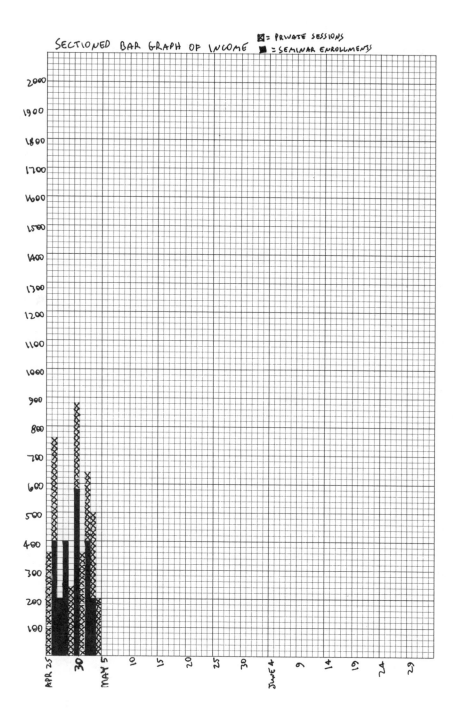

SECTIONED BAR GRAPH OF INCOME   ☒ = PRIVATE SESSIONS

☐ = SEMINAR ENROLLMENTS

159

ILLUSTRATION:

PROGRESS PROJECTION GRAPH SHOWING PROGRESS
TOWARD A SAVINGS GOAL:

To make this graph, put time along the x-axis and the value of
your savings account along the y-axis. Start the Y-axis at the bottom
with the present value of your savings account. Choose meaningful
increments and mark these up to the goal you have chosen for
yourself. Mark daily (or possibly weekly) increments along the x-axis
up to the date you have chosen for achieving your goal.

CHART OF SAVINGS FOR INVESTMENT

DATE	DEPOSITS	WITHDRAWALS	BALANCE
APR 25			7975.45
APR 27	131.00		8106.45
APR 28	43.55		8150.00
APR 29	25.00		8175.00
APR 30	90.00		8265.00
MAY 1	35.00		8300.00
MAY 4	142.00		8442.00

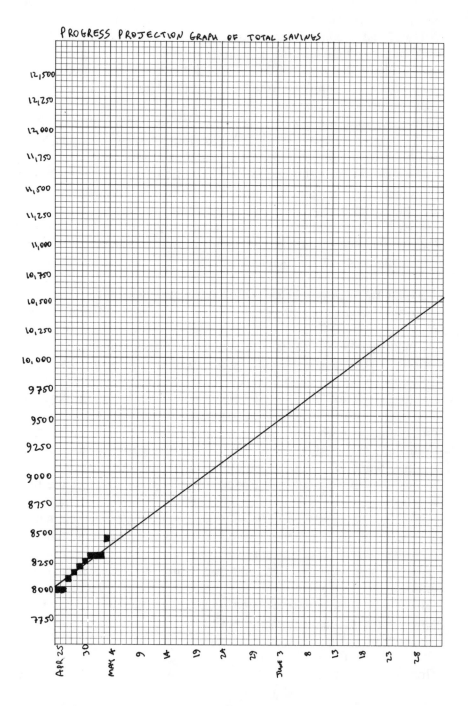

PROGRESS PROJECTION GRAPH OF TOTAL SAVINGS

Now get a straightedge and draw a diagonal line from the lower left up to the square identified by the y-component of your monetary goal and the x-component of you date for achieving it. Each day mark in the actual amount in your savings account. As long as the mark is above the diagonal line, relax. If it is below the line, however, apply whatever technique you have identified for increasing savings more vigorously.

Basically, you choose a monetary goal for some purpose, say $2000 for a vacation. Then you draw a column, several columns wide, usually, from bottom to top on the paper. You write the goal at the top line and zero at the bottom line. You figure out how much each horizontal line is therefore worth and write the amounts on every fifth line going up.

Every time you add money to the account, you round the new total down to the nearest whole increment, draw a horizontal line there, and fill in the chart up to new level.

CUSTOM DESIGNING YOUR OWN MONEY PROJECTS

Money management lends itself exceedingly well to self-improvement projects.

A money project consists of a set of practices designed to achieve a specified goal. The goal could be a purely monetary one, like "save $2000 for a vacation." Or it could be self-improvement kind of objective, such as "find out if tithing will increase my income," or "stop spending frivolously." Or it could be something that is really a combination of both, such as "Become a $1000-a-day salesperson."

You may not want to have a money project going all the time — you may want to take a break after completing one before starting the next one, but I would suggest having one going more of the time than not.

Since money structures vary considerably and are by their nature very personal, I cannot really give you rules to follow in setting one up. Instead I will give you tips and some examples.

All of these assume that you are using a Percentage Budget continuously.

Figure out what sort of problem you are most prone to regarding money. Some common problems include:

Insufficient income

Work you don't like

Too much work

Too little consciousness in your spending

Guilt

Debt

Bad habits of various sorts (drug habits are one example). Remember the adage, "There is nothing as expensive as an expensive bad habit."

Design projects to help you overcome these problems.

Here are some of the ingredients that can go into a money project:

A goal

Discovery Writing

Affirmations (described in chapter 14)

Special charts and graphs

Exercises involving selling

Reading

Other creative practices you make up.

A money project should always have some definite foreseeable ending time. This can be a date or when a particular objective has been reached.

Example A: Suppose your biggest problem is that your income is too low. A good structure might consist of these practices:

1. Every morning and every night write make a Discovery List of "20 Things I could Do to Increase My Income."

2. Make a special savings account for the purpose of accumulating money to invest in business opportunities. This has these rules:

   1. 10% of your income goes in
   2. You can only take money out to invest in something that will probably increase my income.
   3. In any one day you can only take out 50% of what's in there.

3. Keep the following charts:

   1. A daily bar chart of income.
   2. A daily bar chart of the total sales calls you make
   3. A daily high-low-close graph of how much is in your Business Savings account

4. Stick to this structure until your income for four weeks in a row is over $800 per week.

Example B: Suppose your problem is that you spend compulsively and are always going into debt. A good structure might consist of these practices:

1. Destroy all your credit cards.

2. Every day, write a page of the affirmation "It is Ok for me to value saving money more than I value spontaneity from now on."

3. Every day write a Discovery List of "20 Things I Could do to Reduce my Spending."

4. Keep a daily inverted bar graph of total spending.

5. Keep a weekly high-low-close graph of net worth.

6. Stick to this structure until your net worth is above zero continuously for one month.

7. Maintain a sign in your room that says "Consecutive Days of Sticking to My Money Structure."

EXAMPLE C: Suppose your main goal is to get started having some income from self-employment. A good structure might be:

1. Purchase 100 copies of *Your Fondest Dream* from the publisher at a 50% discount and sell at least 5 copies at retail every day.

2. Every day make the following Discovery Writings:

"20 Things I Like About Selling," and

"20 Reasons Why any Sane Person Would Buy a Copy of *Your Fondest Dream*."

3. Start an account for "Self-Employment Investment" into which put 10% of your income.

4. Keep a bar graph of Income from Self-Employment.

5. Read at least one chapter from *How to Master the Art of Selling* every morning.

6. Every night, write down in a journal everything I can think of that I learned about selling that day.

7. Stick to this structure until I've sold all 100 copies of *Your Fondest Dream*.

EXAMPLE D: Suppose you've never been good at saving. A good structure might be:

1. Open an investment savings account at a bank at least three hours drive from anywhere you normally go. Get everything you need to make deposits regularly by mail.

2. Open a large purchases savings account at a bank near you.

3. Put 10% of your income into each account whenever it comes in.

4. Every day, write "20 things I could do to increase my net worth,"

5. Keep a high, low, close chart of your net worth

6. Stay with the structure until you've saved up $5000 in your investment savings account.

MORE HELPFUL HINTS ABOUT MANAGING MONEY CREATIVELY

1. Make up your own system for putting consciousness into your money management. Figure out what things it would be most helpful to keep track of, what kinds of Discovery Writing would help you most, etc., and then do that.

2. Make your money-management system creative and enjoyable.

3. Write a Discovery List of all the characteristics of your ideal money management system.

4. Every day do some kind of Discovery Writing with regards to money.

5. If you have had trouble with money in the past it would be wise to develop some system that requires you to pay a little bit of attention to money once a day.

6. If you are married or are in a partnership with someone, have a meeting about finances once a week. If you have a history of any kind of trouble with money, have a meeting once a day, or as often as you can.

7. Keep a notebook of what you learn about money. Writing down what you learn from experience (or other sources) will greatly aid you in learning quickly. If you follow this simple practice then you will never have to be terribly frustrated if you lose money in a business venture — it simply means that you have "paid" some money to learn a lesson about business; people commonly pay for getting an education about business anyway. The main thing is to learn your lesson well the first time. If you just don't make the same mistake twice you'll be a master of money very quickly no matter how naive you are now.

8. If you think you have chronic problems related to money please consider this: Debtors Anonymous is a support group based on the 12 Steps of Alcoholics Anonymous. I have never been to a Debtors Anonymous meeting myself but I have talked to people who go regularly. It is not just for people whose problem is literally debt; it is for anyone who has had a problem with bad habits with regards to money. If you have had a problem with bad money habits you certainly have nothing to lose by going to a meeting. Look up Debtors

Anonymous in your phone book. If there is no listing there, contact Debtors Anonymous in Manhattan to get some literature sent to you.

9. If you have not had much trouble with money then you may want to pick one day per week to handle all your financial transactions. On that day send out bills, make bank deposits, move money from one account to another, etc.

10. Make a list of all the procedures to follow on your finance day.

11. If you have your own business, use the services of an accountant, at least on a consulting basis, at least at tax time. Any good accountant will save you more than you pay him or her. If you are not an accountant yourself, assume that expert consulting will be beneficial.

12. I definitely recommend that you read *Money is My Friend*, by Phil Laut, repeatedly.

13. Read good books about money and listen to good tapes about money. Take money seminars. The money and time you invest in education and self-improvement for developing a prosperity consciousness will pay you back in a bigger way in the long run than any other investment could.

14. Be patient and give yourself a little while to get used to your new system. It may seem awkward at first but will soon seem completely natural.

In summary, you can make up your own creative ways of managing your money. I suggest that you do your best to make managing your money stimulating, creative, interesting and conscious.

PART III

HOW TO ACCELERATE YOUR CREATIVE PROCESS

Knowing what you want and knowing what to do to get it are not enough to assure you of getting what you want in any endeavor. Psychological and emotional factors always play a huge role. All human beings are very complex creatures and sometimes our complexity makes it seem unreasonably difficult for us to get what we want.

Part III of this book is all about simple, proven methods of aligning your own mind and emotions to increasing your creativity.

CHAPTER 11

YOUR CONTEXTS CREATE
YOUR RESULTS

Your most important freedom is also the one absolute freedom that no one can take from you — your freedom of thought. In the blink of an eye you can choose to look at something in a whole new way. You can choose to have a new relationship to any situation, any project, any problem in your life. By changing your relationship to something you can increase (or decrease) your ability to be creative with it.

Every creative breakthrough comes from a change to a more appropriate mental context. This chapter describes the fundamentals of how different ways of relating to things produce different results. Later chapters are about skillful means utilizing these principles.

"Context," "attitude," "way of relating," "point of view," "frame of reference" all mean more or less the same thing. I prefer to use the word "context" most of the time because it is the broadest and because it makes clearest the difference between what you are relating to and how you are relating to it.

The cont*ent* means the thing itself, the situation at hand, what you're dealing with, the direct experience, what actually happened, etc. To quote Sgt. Friday, "Just the facts, Ma'am."

Your cont*ext* determines what that means to you.

For example, suppose your husband or wife leaves you. Is that good or bad? From one context it is awful because it means the end of a dream, big scary changes, etc. From another context it's really quite wonderful because it wasn't working very well anyway, now you have new freedom, etc. Typically in this situation most people start off holding it in a negative context (partly because they still have momentum going for trying to keep the relationship together) but wind up holding it in a positive context and moving on to better things. Almost everyone had the experience of breaking up with their first sweetheart. That was probably very painful at the time, and yet if you're grateful for any of the sweethearts you've had since then you might as well be grateful for breaking up with that first one. Anyway, I doubt that anyone would really want to have all their former lovers following them around everywhere.

A classic example of context is provided by a glass of water. Do you perceive it as being half-empty or half-full? Nothing about the glass of water is affected by how you perceive it but a great deal about you is affected.

If you train yourself to focus your mind on the resources that are actually available to you, rather than making it wrong that some other resources are lacking, you will become consistently more creative.

Sometimes I enjoy solving the kind of "Brain-Buster" logic problems one finds at the back of science magazines. The reason one of these problems is interesting enough to publish is that when you first read it your mind will say "I can't solve this. There's not enough information here." The solution always comes from making a shift of context away from focusing on the information that isn't there that you wish were, to focusing in a positive way on the information that is there. The same principle applies to solving any problem in life.

What you want to do in life is relate to each situation in the way that works the best for dealing with it effectively. The ability to change contexts is a most valuable skill.

When you are working on any project you can always focus either on your distance from the goal or on your nearness to the goal. It is much easier to maintain enthusiasm with the latter point of view.

LIMITATION IS CAUSED BY AN INAPPROPRIATE CHOICE OF CONTEXT

Whether any goal is perceived as possible or impossible, easy or difficult, is a function of the context in which it is held. The march of human progress gives countless examples of this. Every invention and discovery is immediately preceded by a change of context. The discovery of America was immediately preceded by a shift to the context that the shore far to the east could be reached by sailing far enough to the west. The invention of the light bulb was preceded by the shift to the context that something could be sustained in incandescence without it going though combustion. My development of Vivation (see chapter 12) was preceded by a shift to the context that since the result of self-improvement is pleasurable perhaps discarding the uncomfortable part would make the process more efficient.

The search for a solution to any problem can best be thought of as a search for the most appropriate context. "Argue for your limitations and sure enough they're yours," is something that it's very useful to keep in mind.

The origin of all apparent limitation and of all negativity lies in the use of a specific kind of inappropriate context. I call this a "negative" context. I invite you to think carefully about what a negative context is:

A negative context is any context in which you compare what is real (the content) to an imaginary standard and decide that what you're imagining is better than what is real. A jargon term I like to use for that is "make-wrong." When you hold something in a negative context you are "making it wrong." In other words, the content is something that in fact could be either good or bad, depending on how you look at it, and you are choosing to look at it in a way that makes it seem bad.

For example, suppose you're making yourself wrong for not being more successful. The truth is that you could be grateful that you are as successful as you are. But you are comparing yourself to an imaginary standard of how successful you should be and thus you're being negative toward yourself.

Suppose you're visiting a foreign country and you're making it wrong for not having better phone service. You could be grateful that they have phone service at all (not that long ago nobody had phone service) but instead you're comparing their phone service to an imaginary standard and thus you're being negative toward it. Please note that this will probably not be helpful in getting what you want from the operator!

"Imaginary standards" are things like: how it should be, how good things used to be back in the good old days, how you wish it were, what somebody else has, etc. All the "shoulda, coulda, woulda" and all the "if-only's."

Anytime something seems bad, unpleasant, limited, difficult, or impossible it is because you are comparing the reality of how it is to an imaginary standard of how you think it should be. "Compared only to itself" anything is fine and good.

The term "positive context" means any kind of context in which the content is considered as it is instead of compared to an imaginary standard. Understand that "positive context" doesn't mean being all smiley and gleeful about it.

To further illustrate these principles, let's say you have $1,000 and you are upset that you don't have $100,000. You have the option of being happy with what you have. There is no limit to how grateful you can be for the money you've got and there is no limit to how much you can do with it (quite literally, there are infinitely many uses to which you could put it). By focusing on the money you don't have you are comparing what is real to something that is purely imaginary. There is absolutely nothing you can do with the $99,000 you don't have; any real money is infinitely more valuable than all the imaginary money put together! By making your financial situation wrong and thus pulling away from reality you get an experience of suffering and limitation. If you can find a way to switch back to a context of gratitude, then you will not only feel better immediately but your creativity will also be freed up to find valuable uses for your money and ways to make it grow.

Things are not the way people think they should be; for good or ill, things are the way they are. Make-wrong is in every case a painful separation from reality. Any time you are making anything wrong you are not fully in touch with reality because a substantial part of you is contemplating something that is purely imaginary, i.e., how you think it "should" be. The challenge for us humans is to accept reality as it is and focus our minds on how best to use what is real to our benefit. Creative breakthrough comes from focusing on the resources that actually do exist.

Your happiness, your creativity and your ability to serve are all functions of context, not content. The shift to being grateful that things are as good as they are is empowering in every case because you can do something with what actually exists. Make-wrong simply separates your mind from reality and hides from you your ability to make use of what is.

Negative contexts in all cases create the illusion that something is wrong with the content. As long as the person insists on continuing to make the same things wrong, no solution will be found. The mind needs to be freed up by shifting the situation from a negative to a positive context. Only in this way can one gain access one's creativity.

There is enormous power in knowing that it is your mental attitudes that create the results you get in life, because you can change your mental attitudes and thus change your results. You always have a choice about contexts; you never have to stay with a context that is not working for you. Advanced skills of shifting contexts are presented in Chapters 12 through 14.

HOW YOUR CONTEXTS CREATE WHAT HAPPENS IN YOUR LIFE

The mechanism by which your contexts create your results is through three principles: the Interpretive Power of the Mind, the Attractive Power of the Mind, and the Creative Power of the Mind.

The Interpretive Power of the Mind is that if you believe things are a certain way then you will interpret whatever happens as being that way, even though you could interpret it in other ways. For example, if you think someone is always critical of you then they could be complimenting and you would still interpret it as being criticism. Or if you think you're funny then you'll even interpret groans as appreciation of your jokes.

The Attractive Power of the Mind is that if you think things are a certain way then you will attract examples of that. A classic example of this is the tragedy of a person who attracts one abusive relationship after another, typically because they have concluded, based on childhood experience, that that's how relationships are. Or if you believe that you are sexy then you will attract people who think you are sexy.

The Creative Power of the Mind is that if you think things are a certain way you will tend to create them being that way. An example is that if you believe you are accident prone then you will create accidents. Or if you believe that you always succeed in the end then you will create turning even major setbacks into ultimate success.

The three of these principles taken together are called the Law of Increase. The Law of Increase is, "Whatever you focus your mind on tends to increase in your experience."

There are countless examples of the Law of Increase in everyone's life. If you focus on how poor you are you will tend to get more and more poverty. If you focus on how unpopular you are you will tend to become more and more unpopular. If you focus on how good you are at something you will tend to get better and better at it. If you focus on how much you enjoy your work then you will enjoy it more and more as time goes on.

SHIFTING FROM NEGATIVE TO POSITIVE

The shift from a negative context to a positive context is called "integration" because something you had held in opposition to your sense of well-being you now integrate into your sense of well-being. If you are focusing on how awful it is to have only $1000 you are making your money wrong. If you shift to gratitude that you have any money at all you integrate the money back into your sense of well-being again.

All unpleasant emotions come from holding something in negative context. There are two ways to cause emotional resolution. One is to integrate the situation you had the negative emotions about into your sense of well-being. The other is to integrate the emotion itself into your sense of well-being — if you make peace with your feelings about something then you will experience resolution of the emotions. The term "integration" refers to either one of these approaches.

Every experience in life can be integrated. You can find ways to benefit from everything that exists, everything that happens. It is universally to your benefit to do so.

Integration always requires that one cease blaming the content. As long as you tell yourself that your emotional discomfort is caused by the glass being half empty you will not get to realizing that it is the context in which you have been holding the glass of water that has caused all your discomfort.

Each integration is a quantum of personal growth. Personal growth means the process of gaining in happiness and power. It is the shifting of life experiences from negative to positive contexts that enables one to gain in happiness and power. Understanding integration is the most valuable knowledge that there is.

Integration is about harmonizing with the reality of your experience right now. It does not mean giving up on making things become better in the future. In order to get this very important point across I need to explain something about the nature of time.

Everyone has two ways of relating to time. One way is the sense in which the present moment is all that's real — you can only touch the present moment, the "eternal now." This way of relating to time is called "Momentary Time." The other in which everyone relates to time is the sense in which the future and the past are considered real and the flow of time is considered real. This context is called "Linear Time" and it is just as valid and just as important as Momentary Time. Everyone uses both of these all the time and yet the two are very different from one another.

Happiness and love and things like that are purely functions of Momentary Time. You're only happy to the extent that you are happy right now. How good things used to be won't make you happy and neither will hope about the future. Similarly you only love someone if you love them the way they actually are. Loving how they used to be or how you hope they'll turn out when you're done controlling and manipulating them are just not the same thing.

Freedom, power, and creativity are all functions of Linear Time because they all involve doing something. In order to have any of these things you have to have some sense of how you want things to be in the near or distant future so you have the freedom to decide what creative thing to do next in order to manifest your power.

Make-wrong and integration are both products of momentary time. Make-wrong means you're telling yourself that something about the present moment ought to be different from how it is. Integration means you go back to "allowing" the present moment to be the way actually it is. If you like the present moment and you want even more of what you like about the present moment in the future, there is no make-wrong, no negativity, involved in that.

For example, suppose you have $1000 and you notice that you value money. If you decide you want $100,000,000 in the future and you are grateful for the good start you have toward achieving that, there is no make-wrong and you can proceed with your plans enthusiastically. However if you tell yourself that you should already have the $100,000,000 in this moment then you are engaging in the painful separation from reality that we call "make-wrong."

Integration increases motivation. All motivation comes from values, as I explained in Chapter 6. You always get a clearer sense of your own values when you're holding something in a positive context than when you're holding something in a negative context. As an example, suppose you live in San Francisco and become a connoisseur of Chinese food but you also travel a lot and have a problem with

CALVIN AND HOBBES Copyright © 1987
Universal Press Syndicate
Reprinted by permission.

comparing Chinese food in other cities to the Chinese food in San Francisco. This make-wrong comparison process obviously will reduce your enjoyment of Chinese food in other cities.

When you're eating Chinese food that you like you will naturally tend to focus on the details of what you like about it, thus getting a more detailed sense of what you value in Chinese food. When you're eating Chinese food that you're making wrong, all you tend to notice is that it isn't like the Chinese food you have in your mind — you block out the details of how it is and thus get no further education about your values.

Another example is that when you love someone you want to find out everything about them but when you hate someone you don't want to know anything about them — you know too much already.

Getting a clearer sense of your own values in all cases gives you clearer motivation. The more you hold things in positive contexts the more motivated you will be. When people are locked up with negativity they expect the exact opposite to be true. They think things like "If I just give myself a hard enough time about being overweight maybe I'll lose weight." That this common method of trying to increase motivation is totally wrong is made clear by the fact that obese people exist at all. When people love and accept themselves more they are far more likely to lose weight or solve any other personal problem. Each and every integration experience leaves a person feeling more enthusiastic, purposeful and motivated.

It is more important to be able to enjoy what you have than it is to be able to get what you want. Enjoying what you have is also the key to being able to get what you want. So my advice is to cultivate your skill of enjoying every moment as much as possible. This is the skill of Vivation which is described in Chapter 12.

Experientially, integration is like different things at different times. Sometimes integration is like a mini-enlightenment — a big "Aha!" experience. Other times it's like lightening up — a big "Ha Ha!" experience. Sometimes you can feel the emotional energy you had been experiencing as unpleasant suddenly become a big source of pleasure. Other times something will cease to be an issue so completely that you'll forget that it ever was an issue.

Forgiveness is an excellent example of integration. When you forgive you expand your context of compassion to include the person you are forgiving. You cease insisting that the person "should" be different and allow the person to be a human being and your peer. All the benefits of integration then ensue. Your mind, your emotions and your creativity will free up some. It is never really to your benefit to persist in making someone wrong; however, while you are still making the person wrong it will usually seem to you like it is to your benefit to continue doing so.

Integration is the experience of discovering a new source of benefit and pleasure, a new resource within yourself. It comes about by becoming aware of emotions, physical sensations and other parts of your experience that you have resisted and suppressed and by then expanding your sense of enjoyment, benefit, and acceptance to include all of them. It makes you happier about being human. It also makes you markedly more effective at getting what you truly want from life, because it eliminates internal conflicts.

Emotional integration is the process by which emotions reach a point of resolution. Integration means that you can contemplate the things you formerly had negative emotions about and now have an experience of gratitude. Everyone has experienced integration — anyone who has ever had an experience that was unpleasant at the time i t was happening but can look back on it and see that it worked out for the best has had the kind of change of context that integration is.

Integration profoundly changes the experience of emotion — indeed it profoundly alters the way one perceives everything.

You can influence the content of the future, but all of the past, and indeed this present moment, already are the way they are, and you have no control over their content. You do have control over the effect that your past and present have on you, though. You have control over the context in which you hold everything, past, present and future. Context is what determines the effect the content of an experience has on you.

Integration means making peace with reality. It means allowing reality to make a contribution to you.

I'm not advocating "positive thinking" in the same sense that many people do. Hope is not the point here, nor is faith, though these things clearly have their places. I'm not talking about anything like going into a new business telling yourself that it's impossible to lose money. I'm talking about looking squarely at the present moment reality of your situation and finding a positive way of relating to that.

Although integration often happens spontaneously and everyone has experienced integration many times, most people who don't know any technique for causing integration make things wrong and suppress far more often than they integrate, thus building up a slush fund of suppressed negative emotion over a period of time. It is very wise to learn as much about integration as possible and to take full responsibility for causing integration.

Once a person has decided that something is "bad" or "lacking" in some way, it is often difficult for them to switch contexts and see what is good about it.

There are many ways to cause an experience to integrate. The most efficient method, by far, is Vivation, which is described in the next chapter.

HOW CONTEXT AFFECTS CREATIVITY

Generally what inhibits creativity is make-wrong. I shall present several ways in which make-wrong inhibits creativity. In every one of the cases integration restores the ability to function creatively.

The initial stages of creativity always involve putting thoughts together in new ways. This is easy to do unless you insist too stubbornly on thinking about things in old ways.

People naturally tend to stay stuck in negative contexts because of suppression. It's more comfortable, in a way, to focus on the lofty experience of how things would be in an ideal world than it is to focus on how things actually are in the real world. Negativity and suppression always lock the mind up and limit creativity.

For example, have you ever watched your behavior when you were in a hurry to get out of the house but you could not find your car keys? If you are like most people, during the acute phase of "frustrated search mode" you will follow a repeating pattern, continuing to look for them where they "should" be, even when you already looked there and did not find them. When your mind is bound up with how something should be it is out of touch with reality the way it is, at least temporarily. Anything that facilitates you in accepting your situation the way it is will not only reduce your frustration but will also increase your creativity at once. Once it is OK with you that your car keys are not where you wish they were, then it will be much easier to use your creativity to think of other possible places where they might be.

The first step in effective problem solving is to make it OK with you that the problem is there to be solved. If the problem has been frustrating you then it will be necessary for you to change your mind about it. Learning to integrate at will is very valuable if you have use for a free mind.

If you hold a problem in the context that it is awful and unsolvable, then even if there is a solution it will be very difficult for you to find it. When you are holding the situation in a positive context you will naturally be aware of the resources that you do have for solving it instead of dwelling only on how you wish it were different.

As I already pointed out, you can't be in touch with reality fully while holding something in a negative context. If you're not in touch with reality you can't solve a problem very readily. Instead your mind will keep going around and around about how much better off you'd be if only the problem didn't exist, which is totally unproductive. Making it wrong that you got a flat tire won't get the tire changed nearly as readily as being grateful you've got a spare and a working knowledge of lug nuts.

Make-wrong is what causes people to be motivated by compulsion or suppressive discipline. Compulsions are caused by suppressed emotions creating cross-current desires for relief. Suppressive discipline exists as a backlash against these cross-current desires. Integration allows motivation by enthusiasm.

When you're working on a creative project sometimes thoughts and feelings will get activated that you are not comfortable with. Knowing how to integrate your emotions, especially by using Vivation, enables you to resolve the emotions on the spot by eliminating the negative contexts that are causing them.

Without knowing how to integrate emotions people commonly get stopped in the midst of creative projects when their emotions come up. When this happens people tend to blame the emotion. An example is someone who says "My fear keeps me from becoming self-employed." This is just another example of "blaming the content." Fear cannot stop you from doing anything. Thinking that the fear needs to go away first will stop you dead in your tracks. If you wait for your fear to go away before starting self-employment or jumping off the high dive you will simply stay stuck in your job or stay stuck way up there on the high dive looking like a goat. If you can integrate your fears into alertness and excitement you can proceed in grand style.

A note on structure and flexibility. What I mean by "structure" is anything you create to control your present and future activities so as to assure a particular desired result. A budget is an example. A diet is a structure and so is marriage. Planning the best route to take when driving somewhere is yet another example of a structure. When you make a plan, or a structure of any kind, it is important to acknowledge that reality is not going to fit your plan perfectly. You may take a wrong turn, you might run out of money and break your budget, you might pig out and blow your diet, your spouse might have an affair, etc. Don't let this discourage you about structure. Learn to have a good plan and to integrate the differences between what you plan and what actually happens. Stay fixed on the goal and be flexible about the method. This is the recipe for a happy productive life.

In summary, your creativity or lack of creativity in any situation is a result of the context in which you hold that situation. By adopting the appropriate context there is no limit to how creative you can be when dealing with anything.

CHAPTER 12

CREATIVITY AND FEELING

In the previous chapter I described how making a shift to a positive context gives you access to the power of creativity by focusing your mind on your available resources. In this chapter I describe the most efficient way of making that shift — by making it at the feeling level.

You have feelings about everything. You feel different when you are holding something in a negative context than when you are holding the same thing in a positive context. You can use that difference in feeling profoundly to your advantage.

If you shift from a negative to a positive context mentally, the feeling shifts from unpleasant to pleasant at the same moment. A much more important thing to understand is that *if you shift the context in which you hold the feeling, that will shift the mental context.* This principle is nothing short of revolutionary.

Every negative context gives you an experience of limitation; holding something in a negative context means that you are focusing your mind on the aspect of something which you cannot use. Every negative context also creates an unpleasant feeling in your body. Because the feeling is unpleasant it stands out and draw your attention. If you develop the skill of giving that feeling your attention and shifting to a positive way of relating to it, you will also be developing the skill of causing creative breakthrough.

The skill of "tuning in" a feeling and using that to shift to a positive context is a perfected skill that I have taught to many thousands of people throughout the world. The skill is called Vivation.™*

When I developed the Vivation process in 1979 I did not know that I was developing the most effective method of causing creative breakthrough that there could ever be. I developed it as a reliable self-directed method by which people could cause resolution of their own emotions. First, I perfected the process. Next, I perfected teaching it (I can teach any willing person how to gain mastery over the Vivation process in a single weekend seminar). Then, over a period of years, I noticed that with absolute consistency people's creativity increased when they practiced the Vivation process. That is what led to my investigation of creativity and to the writing of this book.

As it turns out, emotional resolution and creative breakthrough are exactly the same thing described in two different ways. The general term I use for that result is "integration" because something that you had thought detracted from your well-being becomes integrated into your well-being. All emotional healing comes about by making peace with reality. All creative breakthrough comes about by aligning your mind to the resources at hand. There is no difference between the two. Every integration makes you feel better immediately and gives you insight into how best to proceed.

VIVATION WORKS AT THE FEELING LEVEL

Improving your ways of relating to things by working at the feeling level is called "kinesthetic processing." "Kinesthetic" is basically a fancy word that means "feeling-level."

*"Vivation" is a service mark of Associated Vivation Professionals. Only presently licensed members of Associated Vivation Professionals are permitted to use the word "Vivation" in advertising.]

Vivation is the skill of focusing on the very specific feeling that you have in your body as the result of a make-wrong and making peace with it. It expands the experience of peace and self-acceptance in the most direct way possible. It eliminates make-wrong, unpleasantness and mental stuckness with astonishing efficiency. Nothing so honest has ever been so gentle and pleasurable!

I have identified seven major benefits that Vivation has because it is kinesthetic, that even the finest mental process does not have:

1. Immediacy. Because it is kinesthetic, Vivation gives immediate access to suppressed negativity and immediate integration, emotional resolution and creative breakthrough. Feeling is immediate and thinking is not. Processing anything mentally requires time, even at its best, because one word (or one thought) comes after another — thinking is a linear process, feeling is not. Mental processing also has the potential of taking a very long time indeed, as anyone who has spent years in talking therapy knows. Kinesthetic processing is not time-dependent at all, however. You can feel your feelings about something in a single moment. Integration itself is always as quick as shifting from seeing the glass as half-empty to seeing it as half-full.

2. Precision. Vivation always gives access to precisely the negative context that is most standing in the way of creative progress. Because people tend to go into denial and suppression with things with which they are uncomfortable, they usually talk around what is bothering them. They even avoid thinking about it! It is very difficult, even for skillful therapists, to get to the exact erroneous context that is causing a specific problem. With Vivation you can gain access to the exact context that needs to shift because it creates a feeling that stands out in the body. The thought hides from exploration and the feeling stands out for exploration — it's as simple as that.

3. Honesty. Kinesthetic processing is inherently honest. You can lie to yourself in your mind for years at a time, as you may have noticed. In processing kinesthetically, however, you always have your true, honest feeling. Even if you've been lying to yourself mentally, or telling yourself that you don't feel anything, the feeling has a way of bursting through — sometimes when you least expect it. In Vivation we teach people the refined skill of tuning in feelings to experience them as richly and as honestly as possible.

4. Certainty. In Vivation you can feel the result happen with great certainty because integration is an unmistakable experience. You can

feel integration happen. Processing mentally can often leave you with lingering doubts about whether you have really processed the right thing and processed it adequately to get the result you're after. When you are focusing your attention right on the most prominent feeling in your body, however, you can feel the exact moment that it integrates.

5. Autonomy. You are always in charge of your own Vivation process. Once you learn to Vive you can Vive without assistance anytime, anywhere, *even while engaging in other activities simultaneously*!

In trying to use mental processes autonomously you'll always have the problem that the same mind that you are trying to change is the same mind that is directing the process. This can lead to years of wrong turns and blind alleys, due to the mind's natural tendency to defend itself. While it is true that a skillful therapist can greatly aid in preventing these problems of self-delusion, isn't it good to know that you don't have to be dependent on someone else for your own processing? Obviously therapy is not very portable either.

Because Vivation is kinesthetic it bypasses the problems of mental methods. The feeling that comes up when you're confronted with a problem is exactly the right feeling to focus on and integrate in order to have a creative breakthrough — no mental self-defense interferes. Integrating the feeling is no problem once you have acquired the skill: the same skill integrates any negative feeling. Also the feeling continues to feel negative until you actually integrate it — with mental methods your mind will tell you that it has changed when it really hasn't.

6. Built-in quality control. Vivation always processes you toward positivity, love, self-honesty, practicality, creativity and joy, by its very nature. A person can start off very deficient in these qualities and, over a period of time, will reliably develop them simply from Viving. A mental self-help process, by contrast, requires that a person already have a substantial measure of these qualities at the outset or else be at substantial risk of reinforcing the pre-existing states of negativity and self-delusion.

Vivation is inherently honest, as I already mentioned, because when you Vive what you do is focus on the honest feeling that you already have. Vivation is inherently positive because you keep opening up to having a positive experience with each feeling until you feel it transform into peace. There is a price to pay for every negative context — unpleasantness. More than any other process, Vivation gives you an honest (yet gentle) experience of the price you pay for your negativity.

I want to give an example to illustrate this point. Take the case of a workaholic who is in denial about being workaholic. It is very possible that what this person has in his or her conscious mind most of the time is "I can't get enough done. If only I could get more done each day." An example of a mental self-help technique with no built-in quality control is Affirmations (which can be excellent; I describe how to use them in Chapter 14.) This workaholic person may well work with affirmations such as "Every day I accomplish more than the day before," "My work gives me energy and reduces my need for sleep," "I am always alert and purposeful," etc. These might be excellent affirmations in some ways but they reinforce the person's problem. In a Vivation session, however, this person's feelings of frustration about not getting enough done would come up and integrate. By making peace with the feelings of frustration (which could have their origin in childhood or even birth) the compulsion to work in order to suppress them is eliminated. Trying to convince a workaholic to relax can be very difficult. Integrating the feelings that run the compulsion is easy and straightforward with Vivation, however.

7. A kinesthetic process lends itself extremely well to energy-level enhancement of access to the subconscious. The physical body is, above all, an energy system. This is well established and understood not only in Eastern physiological systems, such as acupuncture, but in Western medicine as well (e.g., *Energy Medicine*, a medical textbook by Laurence Badgley, M.D.). The feelings in the body (emotions and other feelings) are configurations of energy. In Vivation we teach a method of modulating the breathing to make wave-like movements of energy in the body that make it much easier to feel the subtle details of feelings. Circular Breathing, as this aspect of the technique is called, makes it possible for even very suppressed people, who normally report no contact with their own emotions, to experience their feelings richly, honestly and pleasurably. We teach people how to make adjustments to the breathing in order to develop and maintain rapport with the feelings as they come up. Circular Breathing is not hyperventilation and Vivation is not a cathartic process nor a process of confrontation. It is a process of relaxing, feeling honestly, and making peace with oneself.

Kinesthetic processing allows material to be integrated very effectively even when it has not been sorted out mentally or described in words at all. Although profound understanding naturally develops as a result of integration, integration is not mainly a process of understanding mentally. Conscious and subconscious negativity can be permanently and completed resolved without ever understanding the material cognitively.

Learning to embrace made-wrong and suppressed feelings is probably the most valuable tool of physical, mental, emotional and spiritual purification you could ever learn. It is a very direct way to extend your context of unconditional love to all parts of yourself, to other people and indeed to all parts of your experience. This expansion of positive contexts not only makes you feel better immediately, it also clears your mind and frees up creativity and effectiveness.

WHAT VIVATION DOES

Every make-wrong produces an unpleasant feeling in the body. It's easy for you to verify this for yourself: just notice how you feel next time you're making something wrong.

These unpleasant feelings tend to become suppressed in the body (corresponding negative thoughts are suppressed into the unconscious part of the mind), where they are not experienced consciously until something in life reminds the person of the negative context they have been trying to keep suppressed. Then the unpleasant feeling comes right back to the person's attention again.

While the feeling is being experienced consciously the person has the opportunity to integrate the feeling or to rethink his or her context about the situation and shift to a positive context mentally. Doing either eliminates the negative context at its source.

In most cases, however, people blame the unpleasantness they experience on whatever (or whomever) has just reactivated their suppressed negative emotions — "Blaming the content," I like to call that. They effort to control the situation and people involved (engage in an unconsciously motivated compulsive reaction, in other words) in order to get the unpleasant emotions re-suppressed as soon as possible. Once they succeed at resuppressing, they go back to being walking time bombs of emotions, hoping against hope that the world will cooperate with their self-delusion. Around and around this emotional merry-go-round turns.

Vivation stops this vicious cycle. By voluntarily welcoming the suppressed feelings the compulsive motivation to avoid them is eliminated. Because Vivation is both gentle and self-directed it is easy to allow feelings to come up and integrate, regardless of how long they have been dreaded and avoided.

In general, whatever gets integrated in a completed Vivation session stays integrated (although make-wrong is an eternal option that goes with having a mind). Nonetheless not all your make-wrongs will get integrated in one session or even in several sessions. The bad news is that if you are like most normal human beings you have thousands of make-wrongs suppressed in your unconscious mind.

The good news is two-fold: every integration feels wonderful and every integration makes the next integration easier.

As you Vive, whatever has been interfering with your ability to fully enjoy your aliveness comes to your attention, feeling-by-feeling, and is transformed, integrated. After a few minutes or at most a few hours of integrating the feelings there comes "completion" — the magical moment when there is no more block against enjoyment and you feel the profoundly ecstatic, detailed joy of aliveness itself.

The effect of Vivation over a period of time is that layer after layer of suppressed negative emotion gets resolved, never to trouble you again. You become much more comfortable with being human. Your self-esteem, relationships, prosperity and creativity all improve dramatically. Many people experience Vivation as a deep opening to their innate spirituality.

Putting all that together, Vivation consists of utilizing skillful means to attain inner harmony, particularly with those things that have produced troubled feelings in the past.

HOW VIVATION WORKS

Above all, Vivation is a *skill*. When you go to a Vivation Professional to learn the process, you won't just get facilitated in a having a healing experience. You will indeed have a profound healing experience — a complete Vivation session. Your Vivation process will facilitate you in integrating very important suppressed negative material and your life will change as a result. But more important than all that, *your Vivation Professional will teach you how to Vive autonomously.* A Vivation session is a learning experience as much as a healing experience.

You, the Viver, cause all the result in your session. No one can do it for you. Only you can allow your suppressed material to come up and only you can focus your awareness on it. Only you can make the decision to stop making it wrong and accept it. It is your development of the skills of Vivation that determines how much and how rapidly you benefit from doing it.

So what are these skills?

Vivation is a single process that can best be taught in terms of five components. These are called "The Five Elements of Vivation."

1. Circular Breathing
2. Complete Relaxation
3. Awareness in Detail
4. Integration into Ecstasy
5. Do Whatever You Do — Willingness is Enough.

Each of these is a skill in its own right and each represents a body of knowledge. You already have skill with each one to some extent and you have the capacity to gain mastery with each. With practice and openness to learning you will progress steadily in learning to apply them. I shall explain each of them to you in some detail.

But first I want to make it clear: Vivation is not five separate processes — it is one process. I know that teaching it as five component skills makes it sound like it's five processes, but it's not; I simply describe it that way because that's the best way to teach you how to master the process. A completely accurate way to describe Vivation that does make it sound like one process is this: *Vivation is the skill of maximizing your enjoyment of the present moment.* That's really all that there is to it. But then a wise person would ask, "Sure, but how do I do that?" I describe it in terms of the Five Elements in order to answer that question.

The Five Elements are not "steps" that you do one at a time — you do them all simultaneously because, in reality, they are all one process.

Now, some detailed explanation of each of the Five Elements.

Circular Breathing is the skill of regulating the flow of life-force energy your body in order to develop and maintain rapport with your feelings. It is a very specific way of breathing that produces a wave-like movement of energy in your body that you can readily feel.

Most of what I write about Vivation is logical, straight-forward and easy to understand, even if you have never done it before. (At least that's my intention!) Without trying the breathing, though, you will never get what it does, no matter how eloquently I describe it. That being said, I'll carry on.

Circular Breathing is not hyperventilation. It is a relaxed, natural way to breathe. It is not the way that people usually breathe, however, and I'll tell you why:

The breath is the main physical regulator of the flow of life-force energy in the body. In order to keep emotions suppressed it is necessary to inhibit the breathing and reduce the flow of energy. This is analogous to turning down a dimmer switch on an electric light. People don't want their made-wrong feelings to glow at them too brightly, so they turn down the power in their body. Circular Breathing doesn't suddenly put your suppressed emotions on high-beam either! What it does is enable you to turn up the brightness ever so gently and gradually until you can "see" a feeling that you've been making wrong, which then gives you the opportunity to integrate it.

The breathing is not the most important of the Five Elements. All that is necessary to integrate an emotion is to feel it and find a positive way of relating to it. You can integrate feelings while you are holding your breath. Circular Breathing greatly facilitates you in gaining access to your feelings and integrating them however.

As long as you are applying all Five Elements reasonably well, it is easy to keep your breathing Circular for hours at a time, because it is a very natural way to breathe. Once you have enough skill with Vivation to be pretty much integrating your feelings all the time, you'll find that your breathing naturally stays Circular pretty much all the time, too, without any conscious attention on your part.

Almost everyone experiences a permanent improvement in their breathing as a result of doing Vivation.

Circular Breathing means any kind of breathing that meets all of the following three criteria:

1. The inhale and exhale are connected together so that there are no pauses anywhere in the breathing.

2. The exhale is completely relaxed and not controlled at all.

3. Either you breathe in and out through the nose or you breathe in and out through the mouth. Inhaling through one and exhaling through the other weakens the effect significantly.

Your Vivation Professional will teach you how to adjust certain variables in your breathing in order to develop and maintain rapport with your feelings. The most important of these variables are the amount of air you take with each breath (which regulates the intensity or subtlety of the feelings) and the speed with which you take the inhale (which regulates the comparative values of the overall pleasure you feel and the specific emotion that is coming up). By learning to adjust these variables you can learn to develop an energy-level rapport with any feeling that you ever experience, be it pleasure, sleepiness, physical pain, or any emotion.

The enhanced energy flow in your body that you get from doing Circular Breathing feels wonderful! It feels great to feel your aliveness in an enhanced way. One of the ways that Vivation benefits from Circular Breathing is that it enables you to feel the pleasurable tingle of aliveness within the very feelings that you have been resisting because you thought that they would be unpleasant. This greatly assists you in integrating the feelings.

There. That's about as clearly and succinctly as I can explain the breathing to you in words. You'll just have to try it out if you want to know more.

Complete Relaxation means what it says — in the presence of your feelings you relax. You don't act the feelings out, you don't tense up and resist them, you don't try to make them go away, you don't even have to talk about them. You just relax and let them be there. Relaxing in the presence of your feelings makes it easier both to feel them and to integrate them.

Awareness in Detail is the skill of focusing in on the feelings as they come up. Your Vivation Professional will teach you the skill of Awareness in Detail primarily with the aid of experiential processes.

Every moment feels like something. Awareness in Detail is the skill of bringing yourself fully into the present moment and allowing yourself to feel the present moment as it is.

As you engage in maximizing your enjoyment of the present moment, whatever feeling is most standing between you and enjoying the present moment infinitely will come to your attention. Awareness in Detail means giving that feeling your attention. You tune the feeling in so well that you notice the subtle changes happening in it from moment to moment.

This "tuning in" enables you to have a thorough experience of the feeling (which is necessary in order to achieve integration) without the feeling having to be intense. It does not work out that more intensity in Vivation causes more result. More thoroughness of attention to the feeling is what does that.

No matter how feeling or unfeeling you may have been in the past, your Vivation Professional can teach you how to gain reliable access to your feelings from now on. The gentleness of the process is what makes that possible.

Integration into Ecstasy is the name I chose for the skill of finding a positive way of relating to a feeling that you have always related to in a negative way in the past. This is much easier to do than you might think. In fact, it's easier to do it than it is *not* to do it. It is easier to be at peace with yourself than it is to be at war with yourself. Integration into Ecstasy is really about getting out of your own way and allowing yourself to experience that even the worst of your feelings don't feel infinitely bad.

"David, you're denying your feelings again, aren't you?"

Drawing by Koren; © 1981 The New Yorker Magazine, inc.
Reprinted by permission.

People talk about their "negative" emotions as though they are awful, but, in fact, commonly seek them out for pleasure. For example, most people would say they don't like feeling afraid, and yet horror movies and amusement parks do billions of dollars of business every year. Similarly if people didn't have the ability to enjoy sadness they wouldn't listen to sad songs. If they didn't like feeling angry they wouldn't watch the news. And so on.

Aliveness itself fundamentally feels good, even if your aliveness is taking the configuration of a "negative" emotion in your body.

Everyone has the ability to enjoy having emotions. Integration into Ecstasy is simply developing that into a refined skill.

Ceasing to make an emotion wrong takes all the unpleasantness out of it. It causes the feeling to integrate into your sense of well-being. Integration into Ecstasy enables you to cause something that had seemed bad to integrate into your sense of well-being. This always gives you a fresh and positive perspective on whatever the feeling was about.

I have personally taught this skill to well over six thousand people, facilitating an average of over ten hours of Vivation for each of them. (Additionally, I have trained several hundred Vivation Professionals to teach this process to their own clients.) Believe me, I have seen a vast range of different feelings come up for people! I have seen hundreds of people successfully apply the skill of Integration into Ecstasy to each of the following: chronic physical pain, memories of being sexually molested as a child, depression, rage, terror, and grief. Needless to say it works on less intense emotional material as well.

You can learn this skill. No matter what private hell you have experienced and no matter what you are suffering with now, you can integrate it.

In Integration into Ecstasy you learn to identify ways that you have shifted experiences from negative to positive in the past and then to expand those ways and broaden them to include more and more experiences.

Different people do this in different ways. I have been collecting the ones that people tell me about for years. At present I have compiled a list of over ninety different ways that people do it. Chapter 13 contains that list.

Remember, every time you shift something from a negative context to a positive context you get a creative breakthrough. Your Vivation

Professional can teach you how to do that with everything that you have ever made wrong.

Do Whatever You Do — Willingness is Enough is about knowing you don't have to do anything "right" in order to achieve integration. Knowing that and trusting that is a skill, albeit a paradoxical one. It is the skill of trusting that everything is evolving as it should be even if you're not in control. Most activities in life do require that you do them right to get the result. In Vivation your willingness to have integration take place matters more than your skill at applying the Elements. Remember that what you are doing is bringing yourself into harmony with reality by ceasing to insist that reality ought to be different from how it is. Letting something be the way it is perfectly natural and does not really involve doing anything right. While Vivation is a skill and an activity and does involve doing, there is a very important sense in which it is about getting out of the way and letting something unusually natural take place. This, the Fifth Element, is essential because it enables you to put your attention on the feeling that is coming up instead of on doing the process right.

So, those are the Five Elements. I'm sure you realize that there's a lot more to each of them than what I have put in this book. Your Vivation Professional will help you to gain mastery over them. At the end of this chapter is a section on how to get started with the process. At the end of this book is a list of Vivation Professionals and a toll-free number to call to locate a Vivation Professional in your area.

My first book, *Vivation — The Science of Enjoying All of Your Life*, is readily available in bookstores and provides 300 pages on Vivation and related topics.

It is worth doing anything it takes to learn to Vive. Mastering the Five Elements will make you a master of your own emotions and a master at creativity, too.

SOME ALTERNATIVE WAYS TO EXPLAIN HOW VIVATION WORKS

Another way I like to explain how Vivation works is that it gives people concentrated practice at "being here now." People will only "be here now" to the extent that they are willing to experience their feelings honestly. When they aren't willing, they do something to suppress awareness of the uncomfortable feelings. The feelings continue to be there but the person pretends that they aren't. In order to stay truly present one must have some method of embracing all of one's emotions. Any emotion, when embraced, transforms into a pleasurable and positive relationship to reality.

Yet another way I like to explain it is that Vivation is a kind of meditation in which you meditate on how good your most unpleasant feelings feel. What a refreshing change from meditating on how bad they feel!

Here's a way I like to explain Vivation in a spiritual context: Vivation is a meditation in which you experience the Divine with the mundane. Most meditations are about seeking God in the same way, in the same place, day after day. Well and good, that certainly seems logical, and works fine, obviously. Vivation, on the other hand, is about finding the presence of God where you would least expect to find it — right inside the feelings you've been resisting the most. To my way of thinking this is the most direct way imaginable to expand one's contact with God in day-to-day life.

SOME FURTHER NOTES ON VIVATION

The same Five Elements work on everything. All it takes to cause emotional resolution is to let your feelings come up in an honest way and find a positive way of relating to them. The same exact skills integrate guilt as integrate shyness. The same skills integrate loneliness as integrate frustration. You can apply them equally well to grief about leaving a relationship as to apprehension about starting a new job. The skill are absolutely universal.

The Five Elements are all that there is to this process. You don't need anything at all to enhance it. For example, you don't need someone who claims to be "clear" to point out your patterns to you, you don't need having something done to you to activate your feelings, you don't need to figure out your birth trauma, you don't need to be kept in isolation and sleep deprivation in order to make all your emotions really raw first, you don't need hot tubs, you don't need affirmations, or anything else. Those things are all fine in their place, but I want you to know that you don't need them.

Any problem that anybody has with learning the Vivation process can be solved by improving their skill with one or more of the Five Elements.

Vivation does not ever need to be intense. No matter how intense anything is when it goes into suppression it can always be integrated at a subtle level of manifestation in a Vivation session. On the other hand, some of us *like* intensity. You can adjust the breathing during your session to give yourself whatever level of intensity or subtlety suits you personally.

As far as I know, Vivation is perfectly safe. I've never known anybody to have any significant problem with it, physically, mentally, emotionally or spiritually. I can't guarantee that nobody ever will — that's not up to me. I'd be surprised if anybody ever did though, because all there is to Vivation is the Five Elements, and none of them are dangerous. There's nothing dangerous about this kind of breathing. There's nothing dangerous about relaxing. There's nothing dangerous about being honest with yourself about your feelings. There's nothing dangerous about relating to your feelings in a positive way. And there's nothing dangerous about trusting that your willingness to make peace with everything will carry you through.

Vivation Professionals teach each new client how to use the Five Elements before beginning the first session. This facilitates making the results rapid and very pleasurable.

HOW VIVATION AFFECTS EMOTIONS

Although Vivation deals with more than just emotions, it works at the same level of your being as where you experience your emotions — at the interface between mind and body. Vivation works on integrating emotions in the most direct way possible. You simply focus on the emotion you're feeling and find a positive way of relating to that.

Emotions are the feelings you get in your body in response to the way you think about things.

Your emotions are determined by the contexts in which you relate to things. When you change contexts, the emotion you have about it changes right then.

There are three primary "negative" emotions. (I'm not calling them "negative" because there is anything wrong with having them, I'm calling them that because they are based on holding something in a negative context.) These three are fear, sadness and anger. Let's explore what type of context causes each one and what happens to each one when it integrates.

Where this information came from initially was from leading self-improvement seminars in Hollywood, where inevitably we would get many people from the performing arts in the seminars. When we talked about emotions stage fright would often come up as a topic.

The experienced performers invariably said that their stage fright never went away, they learned to welcome it because it helps them to give a better performance. I started paying attention to what happens with my own experience of stage fright and what I found was that stage fright and excitement had the exactly the same pattern of energy in the body. The only difference is that if I make it wrong I experience it as fear and if I welcome it I experience it as excitement.

Vivation is the skill of focusing on a feeling you've been making wrong and then welcoming it. By doing this you can feel the feeling integrate and you eliminate negativity, working at the feeling level. For example you can focus on a feeling of fear, apply the technique to it, and at once feel it transform into purely pleasurable excitement.

Fear comes from anticipating a made-wrong future possibility. For example, if you are afraid of death it is because you both believe that you will die and make death wrong. If you either cease believing you will die or stop making death wrong, you will no longer fear death.

There are two kinds of fear, that could be called "rational fear" and "irrational fear". Rational fear means that there really is something to be afraid of — something to engage yourself in preventing from happening . Irrational fear is when the fear is there but there isn't any real danger, even though your body is reacting as though there were something to be afraid of. As an example of rational fear, if you are riding in a car with a drunken driver who is driving erratically at 90 miles per hour, you really have something to be afraid of and the fear exists to engage you in doing something about it — talking him into pulling over and letting you out or whatever else your creativity can come up with. As an example of irrational fear, consider the fear of public speaking. Studies show that speaking in public is what people are the most afraid of. Fear #2 is nuclear war and fear #3 is death. This is in spite of the fact that the mortality rate among public speakers is very low.

Rational fear integrates into alertness and irrational fear integrates into excitement. The purpose of fear is to make you more alert. It actually lowers the threshold of sound that you can hear and improves the acuity of your sight and other senses. It prepares your body to take action. If you are resisting your fear you won't get these benefits so readily, however.

Irrational fear integrates into excitement. Excitement has the same pattern of energy in the body as fear. Adrenalin is the main feeling of both. If you resist the adrenalin feeling you'll get fear, if you accept it you'll get excitement.

Sadness comes from believing that your ability to experience something dear to you is limited. Sadness is often about the past. For example, if you are sad that your beloved dog died it is because your dog is dear to you and you are experiencing the limit to how much you are able to experience your dog. Sadness can also be about the present or the future. For instance you can feel sad thinking that a friend of yours is going to be moving out of town in a few months. You could feel sad wishing you could eat more desserts without gaining weight or wishing you could drink more without getting sick.

Sadness integrates into gratitude. Suppose someone dear to you has just died. What you are left with is your memories of being with that person. If you make it wrong that you have the memories instead of the person in three dimensions, you'll feel sad. If you allow yourself to enjoy the memories you'll have gratitude that you ever knew the person.

Anger comes from making it wrong that you have to do something in order for things to be acceptable to you.

Anger integrates into intention or determination. Anger comes up when there is something you feel you must do and you wish it weren't your role to do it.

For example, suppose you live with other people and you go into the kitchen to make dinner and the whole kitchen is a big mess with dirty dishes and pots and pans everywhere. One way to describe this situation is that your intention to make dinner now needs to include intention to do the dishes first. If you make it wrong that the situation demands that it be your role to do the dishes, then you'll be very angry. But if you let yourself be in harmony with having that task at hand then instead of being angry you'll have simple intention to get the dishes done quickly and get on with making dinner.

For another example, suppose someone insults you. Assuming that you have some degree of self-esteem you won't just stand there and take it — you'll do something to stop being insulted. If this process of doing something is OK with you then you'll have simple intention to just walk away or tell the person you insist on being treated better or whatever. If you make it wrong that you have to do something just in order to not be insulted, then you'll get angry.

All the other emotions are mixtures of these three or combinations of one or more of these three with some particular kind of thought.

Frustration, for example, is a mixture of anger and sadness. It comes about by a combination of thinking you have to do something in order to be OK and thinking your ability to do it is limited. An example is trying to get out of the house to go somewhere and not being able to find your keys. The combination of making it wrong that you can't just leave when you want, that you have to find your keys first, and making it wrong that your ability to find your keys is limited, produces a profound feeling of frustration. Integration of frustration leads to grateful intention — enthusiasm.

Jealousy, as another example, has components of all three primary emotions plus the thought that someone else is having more fun than you are and that's not OK.

People talk about their emotions as they don't enjoy them and they act as though they do enjoy them. If you were to take a clip board and go down to the main business intersection in your town at noon on a workday and ask the passersby "Do you like fear" the vast majority would say "NO". Nonetheless, amusement parks and scary movies do billions of dollars of business in the United States every year. The only reason to go to a roller coaster or a scary movie is to get a pleasurable experience of fear. Even if you don't engage in these activities you must admit that the fact that so many people do engage in these activities proves that there is nothing inherently unenjoyable about fear.

Similarly if people didn't enjoy their feelings of sadness they wouldn't listen to sad songs and if they didn't enjoy their feelings of anger they wouldn't watch the news.

Obviously emotions are more enjoyable than their reputation would lead you to believe. Making emotions wrong causes them to stay stuck. If you switch to allowing the sensation of an emotion to be pleasurable, the emotion integrates and whatever the emotion was about is shifted to a positive context.

The reverse process works just as well. If you focus your mind on something you've been having unpleasant feelings about and mentally shift that to a positive context, the unpleasant feelings will immediately disappear and you'll have pleasant feelings when you think about that same thing.

It is actually easier to integrate than it is to make wrong. It is easier to focus on what is there than to focus on what isn't there. Emotional peace is a more stable energy state than emotional turmoil. The main reason people don't integrate more often than they do is because of a phenomenon that is called "suppression" at the feeling level and "denial" at the mental level.

Nobody wants to contemplate something that makes them feel bad. Once someone makes something wrong they do feel bad about it whenever they contemplate it. This gives the person an emotional stake in not thinking about it. This leads to suppressing the feeling and denying that there is a problem. Life itself has its way of bringing problems and emotions back to a person's attention. This gives a person another opportunity to shift to a positive context, to integrate.

Emotions transform but they don't go away. In other words if you start out having negative feelings about something you don't wind up with no feelings about it; you wind up with positive feelings about it.

VIVATION AND CREATIVITY

Creativity means taking the resources at hand and using them to achieve a desirable and original outcome. Vivation greatly enhances a person's conscious awareness of what the resources at hand are. Vivation eliminates the helplessness and apathy that are usually the biggest blocks to creativity. Vivation enhances conscious contact with the unconscious mind, which everyone who has ever dreamed knows to be a vast reservoir of creativity. By eliminating negativity and internal conflict, Vivation frees up a person's creativity in many, many ways. Enhanced creativity is perhaps Vivation's most universal result.

VIVATION AND SELF-ESTEEM

Vivation improves self-esteem in a very direct way. It could be called the skill of learning to love parts of yourself that you had previously been making wrong. Developing unconditional love for yourself (and unconditional love for your experience of life) causes your self-esteem to increase dramatically.

VIVATION AND PROSPERITY

A very, very common experience among people who learn to Vive is that their income goes up and they start doing work that they love. By increasing self-esteem, Vivation naturally leads a person to demand more of what they want from life. Since it also boosts creativity, it is natural for people to become more successful at whatever they do. We have observed for years that a high percentage of people who learn to Vive decide to become self-employed.

VIVATION AND LOVING RELATIONSHIPS

Everyone knows that it's a good idea to be unconditionally loving, few know how to accomplish that. Vivation makes unconditional love possible because it enables you to embrace all your feelings, including the ones that the people around you stimulate just by being the way they are! The enemy of a happy relationship is insisting that your partner should be different from how he or she actually is. When you know how to let your feelings be OK with you, then you also know how to let your partner be OK with you.

Vivation and sex go together very, very well. Consider this: What is there to good sex besides breathing, relaxing, feeling every nuance of sensation in an enhanced way, maximizing enjoyment of every moment and doing whatever you do? We could call them the "Five Elements of Sex" and probably increase enrollment in our seminars. Since the Five Elements also enhance every other aspect of life, however, we have chosen to continue calling them the Five Elements of Vivation.

If you and your partner both learn to Vive, your relationship will very probably become much stronger, happier and more compassionate and supportive.

It also happens sometimes that integrating feelings enables people to realize that it's time to leave a relationship. When this happens, Vivation makes it possible to integrate the feelings of grief, loneliness, anger and guilt that usually come up for people.

VIVATION AND PSYCHOTHERAPY

There many different kinds of psychotherapy and people go to therapists for a variety of reasons. In general, I feel that psychotherapy is one of the most positive developments of the twentieth century. Millions of people are helped every day by psychotherapists.

It is my experience that Vivation works better than anything else when it comes to causing emotional resolution. On the other hand, psychotherapy is indispensable for sorting things out, making decisions, working things out in relationships and hundreds of other applications as well. Vivation is no substitute for psychotherapy.

In the course of teaching many thousands of people all over the world to Vive over the past ten years, my colleagues and I have found that Vivation enhances the effectiveness of psychotherapy. We have never known of a single case where Vivation in any way interfered with any modality of psychotherapy and we hear all the time, from clients and psychotherapists alike, that Vivation has contributed to the progress people make in therapy. This is no surprise at all considering that Vivation very directly enhances a person's contact with his or her feelings while simultaneously enhancing the person's ability to recontextualize. These are important components of most modalities of psychotherapy. The enhanced ability to have access to one's feelings, and the enhanced self-confidence one gains from Vivation in dealing with emotional material, makes all such work go faster.

USING VIVATION IN DAILY LIFE

After a few guided sessions you will be able to Vive by yourself, without further assistance. You will be able to Vive while engaging in the activities of your day-to-day life.

Vivation is an internal process and it doesn't look unusual to other people, so you can even use it when you're in public. Whenever you find yourself in the midst of anything unpleasant you can Vive to integrate your emotions and to enhance your creativity in dealing with the situation. When you are already enjoying yourself you can Vive to bring yourself more into present time and enhance your enjoyment of what already is pleasant.

You can Vive while at work, while playing golf, while making love, while talking on the telephone, or very nearly any other time. This means that in your day-to-day life, your emotions can actually be used to your benefit, and indeed enjoyed, as they arise for whatever reason. Viving while engaging in another activity is called "Vivation in Action." In general, the goal of Vivation Professionals is to develop in each client, as quickly as possible, proficiency to be able to Vive in Action. An intermediate step to that level is the ability of the Viver to lie down and complete a Vivation session without the assistance of the Vivation Professional. This is usually attained within 5-15 sessions.

HOW TO GET STARTED

Vivation is the only process in this book that you can't learn from the book and immediately start using on your own. It is necessary, by the nature of the process itself, to learn from someone who is trained to teach the technique, i.e., from a Vivation Professional. However, even if you never visit a Vivation Professional, reading about the technique will undoubtedly give you insights into how your mind and your emotions work. Simply reading this chapter and the next one will probably enable you to free yourself from some stuck negative feelings.

Vivation is a learned skill and it is extremely valuable to start off with a trained Vivation Professional. Your Vivation Professional will teach you the skills of efficient accessing and efficient integrating of your feelings. It is your development of these skills that makes Vivation effective and pleasurable for you. There are Vivation Professionals all over the world, probably at least one within driving distance of you. I suggest looking in the back of this book first, to see if anyone listed there is near you and then calling up the toll free number to have a more extensive list sent to you.

Although the fees charged by Vivation Professionals vary substantially, I believe you will find that it is not very expensive to learn to Vive from any of them.

You can learn to Vive either in seminars or in private sessions.Either way, your Vivation Professional will start off by teaching you about the Five Elements, probably with a combination of telling you information and having you do some simple experiential processes.

A session with a Vivation Professional almost always consists of learning more about the Five Elements and then doing Vivation itself.

After the instructional part is over (in a private session instruction usually takes about an hour and in a seminar, for very thorough instruction, it might take as long as 5 hours) your actual Vivation session will begin. This is almost always done lying down in the first few sessions, so that there is nothing to do but Vive. In later sessions you might do it differently.

The first few minutes of your first session will probably be about getting used to the breathing and the enhanced energy-flow in the body. Within a few minutes patterns of energy will start emerging and the Vivation Professional will guide you into exploring and integrating these. From the end of the instruction to the point of completion for the session usually takes one to two hours. At the end of each session you will probably experience feeling better than you ever have before.

You'll find that every session is different because the material that you have already integrated is not there to come up in future sessions. The range of feelings that comes up in Vivation is absolutely astonishing!

It is very important to understand that the Viver produces all the results in Vivation — the Vivation Professional does not produce any of the results. Vivation is entirely a self-directed internal process. You get results according to your development of the skills involved. Once you gain some mastery over the skills you will have them available to you forever. Vivation does not create even the initial stages of dependency on the Vivation Professional. Indeed one of the effects of Vivation is an enhanced sense of emotional independence.

It is my advice that you read the first 12 chapters of *Vivation — The Science of Enjoying All of Your Life* prior to having your first session. These chapters explain the process in much greater detail than I have in this chapter and reading them will enable you to learn the process much faster. It is readily available in bookstores, almost all Vivation Professionals keep a supply on hand, and you can also use the convenient order form at the back of this book to order a copy from the publisher.

Vivation is a service mark of our professional organization, Associated Vivation Professionals (AVP). Only people who know the Five Elements, and who sign an agreement to teach the skills of Vivation autonomy to their clients, can join AVP. Only current members of AVP are legally allowed to call what they do "Vivation" in advertising. It is possible that you might run into someone who does some other kind of work with clients but will make the false claim that what they do is the same thing as Vivation. Such people do not have the skill of teaching you to use the Five Elements on your own. Even if what they are doing is otherwise good, their claim that what they are doing is the same as Vivation shows them to be lacking in integrity. You will do much better to go to a genuine Vivation Professional who is a current member of AVP.

Generally speaking, Vivation Professionals teach people to Vive in one or more of these three ways: 1. In private sessions, 2. In short seminars, 3. In Vivation Professional Trainings.

Private sessions have the advantages of complete privacy and of getting the full attention of the Vivation Professional. This is the best method for those who feel a need for either of these specific benefits. Naturally, this also tends to be the most expensive method.

Short seminars, typically a Friday evening, whole Saturday and whole Sunday, give more in-depth understanding of how to apply the Five Elements. They also give the benefits of group interaction. These usually provide the most cost effective way to learn Vivation.

Vivation Professional Training is obviously suitable for those who wish to become Vivation Professionals, but is also suitable for those who want in-depth experience for their own personal use. Topics closely related to Vivation are covered in depth also.

I, myself, teach Vivation in all of the above formats. I travel all over the world leading weekend seminars — this is the work I do most. I give a few private sessions both when I'm home and during my travels. My colleagues and I lead Vivation Professional Trainings two to three times per year in the United States, and occasionally in other countries.

I invite you to contact me, personally, about any aspect of this work. I lead seminars on Vivation and seminars on creativity constantly. If you are interested in attending one of these seminars or interested in producing a seminar for me in your city (a lucrative business opportunity), please call me or write to me. I am also particularly interested in participating in well thought out scientific research on Vivation. Complete information about contacting me is in the back of this book.

CHAPTER 13

HOW TO BE EMPOWERED BY EVERYTHING

This chapter presents simple techniques for shifting any experience from a negative context to a positive context. The basic understanding of contexts, negative and positive, is conveyed in Chapter 11. I suggest you make sure you have read that chapter before reading this one.

These techniques are part of the skills Vivation Professionals teach their clients in the Fourth Element, Integration into Ecstasy. Therefore these are often called "Fourth Element Techniques."

Everyone has had experiences of this kind of recontextualization. Everyone has had experiences start off seeming bad and, because of a change of consciousness, wind up being obviously good. Fourth Element techniques came about through observation of people in the midst of making that shift. I have been collecting these for years. At this writing I have identified one hundred ways that people shift contexts — which happens to be a nice round number but I'm sure I'll keep finding more.

In Vivation we use these contextual shifts at the feeling level. This works because the context in which you hold something determines the quality of feelings that you have about it. Whenever you are making something wrong you have unpleasant feelings about it. If you shift to any kind of a positive context you will then have pleasant feelings about that same thing. There are substantial benefits to learning to work at the feeling level, which are explained in the previous chapter.

You can also use all of these mentally, without learning to use Vivation, and still get a very substantial benefit.

HOW TO SHIFT ANYTHING TO A POSITIVE CONTEXT

I'm going to present these techniques to you in a process. Here's how to do the process:

1. Take out a sheet of paper and make a list of ten things you don't like. Any ten. Notice that when you contemplate them you get a feeling in your body that you don't enjoy.

2. This process consists of putting your list of things you make wrong together with my list of ways to shift to a positive context. Start with the first thing on your list and the first contextual shift on my list. Try out the contextual shift and see if the thing on your list integrates. Either it will or it won't — either way is fine.

3. If it does integrate then go onto both the next thing on your list and the next thing on my list and do it again. If it does not integrate then stay on the same item on your list but try out the next technique on my list. And so on.

The way you can tell if the thing integrates is by paying attention to your feeling about the thing. As long as you have an unpleasant feeling about it you are still making it wrong. If the context shifts, you'll feel better when you contemplate the thing.

Some notes on this process before you begin:

A. These are tools. For an analogy you could pick any tool you could by at a hardware store, say a hammer. What you don't do is buy a hammer, set it down on the table in front of you, cross your arms skeptically and say "OK, now let's see you drive some nails!!" The nature of tools is that they don't really do anything. You do the work, using the tool. The hammer doesn't drive the nails, you drive the nails using the hammer. If you don't have intention to drive the nails, the hammer will be of no use to you.

The same thing applies to these techniques. If you don't intend to shift to a positive context, I'll guarantee that these won't shift it for you. If you do intend to shift contexts, you can use these to accomplish that.

B. This is a very shallow process compared to Vivation. Your feelings about anything are complex. Vivation allows you to integrate all of that complexity because each component of the feeling will come up for you to integrate it. Each integration will activate the next pattern of energy. As long as anything feels out of harmony you keep Vivation into it. You know you're done with a Vivation session when everything feels good.

For the purpose of this process, call it an integration if you feel the energy make a quantum move in the direction of feeling good, even if some of your feelings about it still feel a little unresolved.

C. They are stated here in the rather quirky way that I prefer. It is fine if you want to reword them to suit yourself.

D. The reason there are so many of these is because everyone thinks differently. Not all of these work for anybody. All you need is to find three or four that are especially natural for you to use, perhaps ones that you have used in the past. Then just expand the application of that contextual shift to more and more things.

FOURTH ELEMENT TECHNIQUES
OR
"100 WAYS TO SHIFT ANYTHING TO A POSITIVE CONTEXT"

1. Find a way to enjoy it.
2. Notice that what you are experiencing is not infinitely bad. Be grateful that it's as good as it is.
3. Expand your gratitude for your existence to include the particulars of what you are experiencing now.
4. Surrender to the fact that it is the way it is whether you like it or not.

5. Compare it only to itself.

6. Cultivate a sense of fascination with it — notice that it's at least interesting.

7. Expand your compassion for all people who experience similar things.

8. Be open to it making a contribution to you somehow.

9. Give all parts of yourself unconditional love.

10. Extend unconditional love to all parts of your experience.

11. Turn the whole experience over to God.

12. Acknowledge that whether it's good or bad, pleasant or unpleasant is purely up to the context you choose for it.

13. Appreciate that it is exactly the way it is for only one moment in all of eternity. Enjoy it quick before it integrates.

14. Notice your nearness to your goal and let it be glad that it is your responsibility to get more of what you want in this.

15. Acknowledge that it's obviously the way some part of you wants it to be.

16. Appreciate that it helps you get to know yourself better.

17. Acknowledge that it would be OK to lighten up about it.

18. Imagine what it would be like for it to be exactly the way it is but for you to feel integrated about it.

19. Notice the extent to which you already do feel OK about it.

20. Since you know that it's inevitable that you'll make peace with it eventually, just go ahead and make peace with it now.

21. Enthusiastically exaggerate your feeling.

22. Enjoy the intensity for its own sake.

23. Be comfortable with its familiarity.

24. Be grateful that the right thing is activated.

25. Claim your good from this.

26. Enjoy the newness of this.

27. Be grateful for your ability to feel.

28. Know that by feeling it you are healing it.

29. Notice that what you are experiencing is funny.

30. Honor it as a teacher.

31. Stay open minded about this.

32. Knowing that the Experiencer, which is who you really are, is Ecstatic about this, choose to have your conscious mind be Ecstatic as well.

33. Laugh at the absurdity of making anything wrong.

34. Notice that considering what you did to make it this way, it didn't turn out as badly as it might have.
35. Acknowledge the benefit you are getting from it now.
36. Notice how this strengthens your relationship with God.
37. Notice how this strengthens your character.
38. Notice how this strengthens your determination.
39. Be grateful for what a good story this will make.
40. Close the curtain on your drama.
41. Allow the Holy Spirit to enter your body through your crown chakra and heal all parts of you.
42. Even if it doesn't seem pleasurable, open up to it as though it werepleasurable.
43. Feel the tingle of aliveness within the pattern of energy.
44. Experience every sensation as an instrument of God's love.
45. Notice that it's a miracle that this moment exists at all and bliss out on the miracle of its existence.
46. Trust that God loves you.

Drawing by Koren; © 1981 The New Yorker Magazine, Inc.
Reprinted by permission.

47. Trust that you are strong enough to handle even the worst of this.

48. Realize that it's not as bad as your worst thoughts about it.

49. Command it to be the way it already is.

50. Relax your mind.

51. Be enthusiastic about integrating it.

52. Praise it unconditionally.

53. Pretend that this is easy.

54. Be very gentle, patient and caring with yourself in the presence of the feelings.

55. Know that God's love is unconditional and you are already forgiven.

56. Be grateful that it's coming up at such an appropriate time.

57. Be grateful that it's in your past.

58. Love the part of you that's activated.

59. Notice that the feelings in your body can't be weirder than you are.

60. Let the pleasurable feelings of strength and vigor that are already present in your body help you to integrate this.

61. Experience every sensation as white light or healing energy.

62. Let your love of Vivation expand to include everything that comes up in your session.

63. Let the honesty with which you feel the feelings feel good.

64. Be grateful that you've got something to Vive into.

65. Let the feeling take you on an adventure.

66. Acknowledge that you've struggled with this about long enough and that trying to control it may not your best strategy.

67. Notice that the Creator of the Universe obviously thinks it's supposed to be exactly like this.

68. Let it be just a pattern of energy.

69. Pray about it.

70. Experience this energy as God's own energy.

71. Welcome this opportunity to let go of ego.

72. Acknowledge that you like a little drama and poignancy in your life anyway.

73. Be grateful that you know how to Vive!

74. Notice that the same God who gave you life and every wonderful thing you've ever experienced is in charge of this also.

75. Let this be a metaphor for your entire life.

76. Be grateful that at least you're a classy enough snob to know a poor quality experience when you're having one!

77. Find the presence of God within the feeling.
78. Appreciate the unique beauty of this.
79. Be grateful that this experience lets you know you're alive.
80. Be grateful that you have such marvelous excuses for your negativity.
81. Trust your body.
82. Acknowledge that all is not lost.
83. Trust that everything is evolving perfectly.
84. Trust that, since other people have made it through this, you can, too.
85. Acknowledge that the stuff that's bothering you is not what really matters the most in life anyway.
86. Be grateful for how this experience educates you about your own values.
87. Welcome the challenge.
88. Notice that if you're doing your best that's the best you can do anyway.
89. Trust in the inevitability of integration.
90. Experience that you love yourself enough to see this through.
91. Just choose love.
92. Acknowledge that perpetuating your negativity about this would not be worth what it would cost you.
93. Surrender to the fact that you just can't win a war against your own feelings.
94. Love the energy in your body unconditionally.
95. Laugh at the brilliant suppressive suggestions of your mind.
96. Be grateful that the part of your body where you feel this activation exists at all.
97. If you can't make it better, then try making it worse.
98. Be grateful that what's happening now is leading up to your next wonderful experience.
99. Make peace with everything.
100. Enjoy this because it's the only life you've actually got.

HOW TO USE THESE TECHNIQUES IN YOUR DAILY LIFE.

Cultivate the skill of pre-selecting and cultivating a positive context. Each morning you can pick out your favorite one of these contextual shifts and use it throughout the day — I call this your "Fourth Element Technique Du Jour." You can write it on a sign or on the back of your hand where you will see it often. It is best to pick, in addition, two or three of the other techniques to use as backups, in case something that comes up doesn't integrate with the main one you're using that day.

With one main one and two or three backups, and the willingness to integrate all of the day's events into Ecstasy, you are certain to have an Ecstatic day.

CHAPTER 14

ATTITUDE BUILDERS

When you know you want to change your attitude about something but it seems like there's a lot of old habits of thought involved, you can make significant progress in building a new attitude by using a technique called "Affirmations."

Affirmations are tools for transforming your habitual ways of thinking. They are similar to "practices" described in Chapter 8, except that where practices are used to build good habits of behavior, affirmations are used to build good habits of thought. Anything that is affected by your thoughts can be affected by using affirmations.

An affirmation is a simple statement of fact stated in a way that is useful to you. The main reason that way of stating the fact will be useful to you is that it is not your usual way of thinking — you use the affirmation to change your usual way of thinking.

Here are some examples of affirmations:

*I love everyone and everyone loves me.

*Obviously I deserve the best of everything.

*My income always exceeds my expenses.

*Obviously I am one of the most creative people ever to walk the Earth.

Some people teach affirmations as though they are magic. They teach that thoughts literally create reality, as though your thoughts change the structures of molecules and atoms. Such people teach that the best way to get a new Mercedes, for instance, is to write thousands of repetitions of something like "I now have a new Mercedes sitting in my driveway," occasionally lifting your head from the paper to peer out the window and see if it has worked yet.

Affirmations do work but not in that way. Affirmations work because you can use them to change contexts. The most important thing in achieving any goal is to hold the goal and the process of achieving the goal in appropriate contexts.

If you contemplate a goal of yours and feel uncomfortable, that is a sign to you that some part of you is holding the goal and/or the process of achieving the goal in an inappropriate context. When you hold a goal in entirely appropriate contexts you feel enthusiastic, not uncomfortable.

If you can discover which inappropriate contexts you have, then you can change those and go from discomfort to enthusiasm. This is the best use of affirmations.

For example, suppose you really do have a goal of having a Mercedes, and your sole source of income is a job that pays you $400 a month. It is likely that when you focus your mind on having a Mercedes some degree of overwhelm will come up. This is a signal to you that you are holding the process in an inappropriate context. You could try the affirmation "All parts of me are enthusiastically setting up my life for me to purchase a new Mercedes."

There are many excellent ways to use affirmations. In this book I shall describe two methods in detail and mention, briefly, several others.

INTERACTIVE AFFIRMATIONS

For this technique, take out paper and follow these instructions:

1. Write the affirmation on the top line.

2. On the next line below, write down whatever objection comes to mind. I like to write the objection (more formally called "the response") in parentheses.

3. On the next line write down a new affirmation that you have made up to handle that negative thought.

4. On the next line write the original affirmation again.

5. Then a new response.

6. Then another new affirmation to handle the response.

7. Then the original affirmation again.

Etc. Etc. Etc.

Do some of the repetitions in the "I" form (first person), some in the "you" form (second person) and some in the "he or she" form (third person).

Here's an example:

*I, Carol, am obviously one of the most beautiful women ever to walk the Earth.

(I'm too short)

*Obviously I am exactly the right height.

I, Carol, am obviously one of the most beautiful women ever to walk the Earth.

(I'm too old)

*Obviously I am exactly the sexiest age.

I, Carol, am obviously one of the most beautiful women ever to walk the Earth.

(I'm too fat)

*Obviously my body is svelte and perfect now and it is becoming even more svelte and perfect very rapidly.

Carol, you are obviously one of the most beautiful women ever to walk the Earth.

(men don't notice me any more)

*All men that I'm attracted to are powerfully attracted to me.

Carol, you are obviously one of the most beautiful women ever to walk the Earth.

(I don't exercise enough)

*I exercise a lot now and I am enthusiastically exercising more and more all the time.

Carol, you are obviously one of the most beautiful women ever to walk the Earth.
(women will be jealous of me and not want to be my friends)
*All women are inspired by my beauty and are strongly attracted to being my friend.
Carol is obviously one of the most beautiful women ever to walk the Earth.
(boy is she ever stuck up!)
*I am humble enough.
Carol is obviously one of the most beautiful women ever to walk the Earth.
(she has such high self-esteem that I feel my low self-esteem in her presence)
*Everyone experiences their own high self-esteem in the presence of me and my high self-esteem.
Carol is obviously one of the most beautiful women ever to walk the Earth.
(the enviable Earth, just to have her walk upon it!)
*It is good that I have a sense of humor about my looks.
I, Carol, am obviously one of the most beautiful women ever to walk the Earth.

This is the method of using affirmations that is best known in the Vivation community. Its main benefit is that by writing down your negative responses you can identify them and change them effectively.

The next technique is one that I developed and have been teaching, almost exclusively, for about two years now. I like it better because it is faster, more efficient and more enjoyable, and it involves creativity. Most people I know who have used Interactive Affirmations for quite some time, prefer this system, too. However, if you are brand new to affirmations I suggest using Interactive Affirmations for a while first, so as to get used to letting responses come up.

AFFIRMATION DISCOVERY

In Affirmation Discovery you don't do any repetitions at all, you make up a new affirmation for each line. This is basically a Discovery Writing of affirmations. Your negative responses get handled automatically in this process because when making up the next affirmation whatever was on your mind while writing the last one will naturally influence how you make up this one. Learn to be very direct in making up affirmations to handle what comes up for you. Go for activating the emotions you have about the subject.

When I give clients affirmations nowadays and I explain Affirmation Discovery to them, I tell them that the affirmations I have given them are starting places. In other words they start with the affirmation I gave them and then make up variations on the theme.

One of the benefits of this method is that in a very short time you will become an absolute wizard at making up new affirmations. Here are some tips on how to make up good affirmations:

1. You can make up an affirmation very easily through the process of "simple inversion." This means that you take whatever the negative thought was, stated simply, and then change the fewest words possible to make it an entirely positive thought. Some examples:

Negative Thought	Positive Affirmation
I feel guilty.	I feel good about myself.
People don't like me.	Everyone likes me.
I don't have enough money.	I have plenty of money.
People rip me off.	Everyone contributes to me.

2. Make your affirmation simple and to the point.

3. Make certain that every component of your affirmation is positive. For instance instead of saying "I don't feel impoverished anymore," you'd do better to say "I feel wealthy all the time nowadays."

4. Make the affirmation impactful. You can tell this best by noticing how you feel when you think the affirmation. If it feels mildly so-so, it isn't very impactful for you. If it makes you feel either really good or really bad, then it is impactful.

5. Make sure the affirmation is different than how you usually think. For instance if you think you do really good work but don't get paid enough for it, there's no point in writing "I do good work." You would do better to write "I make sure I always get paid plenty for my work." If you thought you did crummy work, then "I do good work" would be a fine affirmation.

6. It is often good to put some "amplifier" words in your affirmations. Examples of amplifier words are: always, obviously, absolutely, best, most, extremely, etc.

Here are some additional tips on using Affirmation Discovery:

1. Write the affirmations as fast as you can write or type, just like with any other kind of Discovery Writing.

2. Always make each affirmation different by at least one word than the one that preceded it.

3. Try affirmations in the second and third person as well as the first person. For example:

I am good.

Jim, you are very good.

Jim is always very good.

4. Stay on the same main topic until you reach a resolution you can feel.

5. Unlike other forms of Discovery Writing, with Affirmation Discovery you don't need to number your page.

Here are some of the advantages I have found to using this method instead of doing repetitions:

1. This is more like how the mind works. The mind doesn't think its negative thoughts in repetitions. Instead it forms networks of related negative thoughts. Affirmation Discovery creates networks of related positive thoughts, which works much better than repetitions of one positive thought ever could.

2. Repetitions are boring. Because this is creative and dynamic it never gets boring.

3. Because this produces results far more efficiently than repetitions, it lends itself far better to using "on-the-spot" in a troublesome situation.

4. Because it produces results more efficiently it isn't necessary to get disciplined about doing the affirmations every day.

5. Doing Affirmation Discovery will give a person the benefits of expanded creativity in all areas of life that Discovery Writing does. Just writing endless repetitions of affirmations that someone else gave you gives none of this benefit.

6. You don't have to start with the "right" affirmation. By following your emotional responses you can start almost anywhere and wind up using exactly the "right" affirmations by the time you are three of four affirmations into the process.

Here are some of my favorite "starting place" affirmations for a variety of topics:

SELF-ESTEEM

*I love everything about myself.

*I am good.

*Obviously I am one of the finest human beings ever to walk the Earth.

*Everyone loves everything about me whether or not they always want me to know it.

*Everyone is better than everyone else.

*I am ordinary and unique just like everyone else.

MONEY

*I am a master at increasing my income.

*Everyone loves to give me money.

*Obviously I am one of the greatest salesmen ever to walk the Earth.

*Everyone wants what I have to offer.

*My income always exceeds my expenses.

*All parts of me are working enthusiastically to increase my income.

RELATIONSHIPS

*I love everyone and everyone loves me.

*It is natural for me to have a close, loving, intimate relationship.

*I communicate very well with a very wide variety of people.

*My desire is a magnet pulling to me what I desire.

*Women are attracted to me because of my attraction to them.

*Obviously I am one of the sexiest women ever to walk the Earth.

HEALTH

*All parts of me are working together enthusiastically to improve my health all ways.

*Quitting smoking is obviously a lot easier than I thought.

*I am perfectly healthy now and my health is improving rapidly.

*I love getting physical exercise in enjoyable ways.

*I eat what is healthy and my body makes health out of whatever I eat.

*It is OK for me to value my health more than anything else from now on.

Here is an example of what Affirmation Discovery might look like:

I am giving exercising a higher priority than sleeping late.

I always get enough sleep to feel like exercising.

I am willing to exercise every morning whether or not I feel like it.

Exercising in the morning is always one of my favorite pleasures.

The more I exercise the more I like exercising.

I always enjoy getting started exercising again after not exercising for a while.

I am fit and healthy now and I am becoming even more fit and healthy every day.

Exercise supports my safety.

I love the feeling of tiredness I get from exercising.

Exercising is always more invigorating than tiring for me.

Whenever I exercise I always feel better immediately.

Exercise is what I naturally do when I want to feel better.

I feel good now and exercising is sure to make me feel even better.

I always exercise exactly the optimal amount.

I'm glad I'm not a crazy fanatic about exercise anymore.

I only exercise in ways that are completely healthy for me.

Exercising is my number one favorite hobby now.

Here are some other methods of using affirmations. Most of these are described in detail in *Vivation — the Science of Enjoying All of Your Life.* I only want to describe them here and, in some cases, add some updated information. Interactive Affirmations are also described in much greater detail in that book as well.

1. Affirmation Modes. In *Vivation — The Science of Enjoying All of Your Life* is a chapter that contains 101 carefully selected affirmations with a blank in each one to fill in with whatever goal you are working on. You can process your mind very fast and very easily by simply reading aloud all the affirmations, inserting your goal in each one as you go. The Affirmation Modes are designed to handle all the responses you have.

2. Affirmation Proofs. This is a technique in which you do no repetitions at all, you simply identify contexts in which the affirmation is obviously true. Since an affirmation takes effect when your mind accepts it as true, this method is very efficient and direct.

3. Affirmation tapes. If you know some tricks (and how to avoid some traps) you can make excellent progress by recording affirmations on audio cassette and then listening to the tape over and over.

I suggest that you experiment with as many different methods of using affirmations as you can, so you pick the method that is best for you.

Affirmation projects can be extremely effective at changing your mental habits. Here are some tips on utilizing affirmation projects effectively:

1. Always be very clear on what you are trying to accomplish and stay focused on that until you have accomplished it.

2. During a project be certain to do some affirmations every day.

3. Always create a context for negative responses to come up and be handled.

4. There's rarely a good reason to work with the same affirmation for more than one week. At least weekly change the affirmation you're mainly working with.

5. The most thorough affirmation project is called an "Affirmation Diet," which means doing 70 affirmations per day for 7 days in a row. This type of project was invented by Sondra Ray.

6. You can carry a small notebook with you wherever you go so you can write some affirmations while you are waiting here and there.

7. If you learn to Vive you will get better results from your affirmations because you will be better at allowing responses to come up. Using Vivation you can feel the response first and then allow it to come to the conscious thought level. If you know how to Vive, I suggest that you always do Circular Breathing while writing affirmations.

8. Do what it takes to develop excellent facility with the affirmation technique. Affirmations are so versatile and effective that everyone ought to know how to use them.

CHAPTER 15

YOUR PERSONAL CREATIVITY PROGRAM

Creativity, in both its development and its application, lends itself very well to programmed self-improvement. I have been helping people design their own self-improvement programs for ten years now, so I want to offer you some tips. Certainly take what you like and leave the rest.

One of the most important ingredients in a happy life is having some kind of a self-improvement program. All people like to experience themselves getting better. If you don't do any self-improvement at all then you will probably experience yourself getting worse, in a variety of ways, as time goes on — it's unlikely that you will just stay the same. So I urge you to decide what types of self-improvement you like the best and develop a regular program.

By far the best attitude to have about self-improvement is that you do it for the pleasure of doing it. Self-improvement ought to be fun. This is in contrast to the attitude that you do self-improvement because there's something wrong with you and you must do it simply to become as good as normal people. Continuously cultivate a spirit of enthusiasm and you will achieve all your goals much faster.

The purpose of discipline is to create certainty. Especially, in the beginning (but also at important times later), you will probably need some discipline to keep your self-improvement program running smoothly. Commit yourself to doing some effective self-improvement, pertaining to achieving your goals, every day. Probably the more effectively you cultivate your enthusiasm, the less you will need discipline. In any case it is best to cultivate enthusiasm about your discipline and be disciplined about cultivating your enthusiasm.

All the exercises in this book are intended to be used not just once but often, as part of an ongoing self-improvement effort. Clearly the first suggestion I make to you is that you actually do all of the exercises in this book. If you did some of them and skipped others, it is possible that the ones you skipped are the ones from which you would get the most benefit - if your unconscious mind is steering you away from them it could be because some aspect of your negativity doesn't want to be processed.

If you have done all the exercises in this book then you are already well along the way to having a life of continuous and complete satisfaction. Acknowledge yourself for the progress you have made since starting the book. You can use this chapter to help you design a program to achieve your goals as fast and as enjoyably as possible.

INCLUDE THESE THINGS IN YOUR CREATIVITY PROGRAM

Learning to use Vivation (Chapter 12) is the single best thing you can do to enhance your creativity. Vivation will enable you to get much better results from all the other methods described in this book. Many thousands of people, with every imaginable background, the world over have learned to Vive. You can, too. Call the toll-free number in the back of this book to have a list of Vivation Professionals in your area sent to you in the mail.

Be sure that you have a Statement of Purpose that you like, that inspires you, and that feels exactly right for you. This may take several tries with the Purpose Process (Chapter 7) but it is well worth

Copyright © 1981 by Jack Ziegler

Reprinted by permission.

it. Everything else that you do will work better if you are clear about your Purpose in Life.

By knowing your Purpose you can set meaningful goals. Always know what your goals are. Choose them carefully. Having goals that support your Purpose gives meaning a direction to your life and all your activities. It's a good idea to repeat The Goals Process (Chapter 8) whenever it seems like you're entering a new phase of your life — when you have acheived the goals you set last time you did the process, for example.

I suggest doing the Values Process (Chapter 6) every six months or so. I find that the Values Process shows me how I have been changing more clearly than anything else.

I also suggest taking the Creativity Self-Examination (Chapter 2) every six months or so. Cultivating the qualities of creativity (Chapter 3) will increase your creative output enormously and put more joy in your life.

Do some Discovery Writing (Chapter 4) every day without fail. You may well want to do Discovery Writing twice a day. Since each Discovery List of 20 only takes 3 minutes at most, you can never tell yourself you don't have the time to do your Discovery Writing and keep a straight face. Remember that you can use it to solve any kind of problem or to aid you in achieving any kind of goal (Chapter 5).

Be sure to manage your time and your money creatively (Chapters 9 & 10). Don't let yourself slip back into your old ways. By applying creativity to your time and money management, you will increase not only your efficiency with these important aspects of life, but your fun and enjoyment with them as well.Please note that Chapter 10 has detailed notes on developing a self-improvement project specifically regarding money.

If all you do with this entire book is read through the list of ways to shift anything to a positive context (Chapter 13) every day, this alone will greatly increase your happiness and creativity.

You can use Attitude Builders (Chapter 14) to help you process anything that involves your mind. It is worth developing skill with this process because of the extraordinary breadth of its application.

I would also recommend that you try out Creative Visualization. The basic technique is very simple: Relax deeply and then visualize yourself achieving your goal. Get all of your internal "senses" involved: see it, hear it, touch it, feel the emotion of it, even taste something and smell something. This accomplishes more than you might think.

For one thing it makes it real for your mind. If you can't even imagine yourself achieving your goal, you have a long ways to go. When people tell me they "can't even imagine" getting something they want, I always have them imagine it right then. Through the Law of Increase (chapter 11) creative visualization greatly increases your chances for success. For more detailed explanation and more advanced techniques, I suggest reading Creative Visualization, by Shakti Gawain.

When you have decided on a program for building you creativity, I suggest creating a Declaration. This a technique for programming yourself, night and morning, for success. You can use it either first thing when you wake up and last thing before going to sleep or you can use it at the start of each self-improvement session.

Create your Declaration thus:

1. On a sheet of paper, at the top, write, "My Declaration".
2. Next, write out your Statement of Purpose. (Chapter 7)
3. The next paragraph is about your single highest priority goal (Chapter 8). Write, "I will (put your goal in this blank) by (State the specific date by which you want to accomplish this goal.). I already see and feel myself (being, doing, or having the goal)."
4. Next, state clearly and succinctly what you are willing to do to achieve that result, thus: "To achieve this goal I am ing, ing, and ing." (State all the steps in the present progressive tense, including ones that you plan to start in the future.)
5. Finish your Declaration with the following paragraph: "I am absolutely dedicated to achieving this goal in the best and most efficient way. I continuously increase my dedication and I know I will succeed."

FURTHER TIPS ABOUT SETTING UP YOUR CREATIVITY PROGRAM

Demand the space to go through your process: If you are like anybody else I've ever met, there will be times when your mind and your life will seem chaotic to you and those around you. These seemingly chaotic times are of crucial importance to your personal growth because they are times of rapid change. During these times, be supremely compassionate and loving with yourself — and do even more self-improvement. The people around you at work and at home may think it odd that you breathe and write sentences a lot. That's alright — you are doing your self-improvement program for you, not to impress others. It is not necessary to be belligerent or overly demanding with these people, but it is not necessary to take a lot of guff from them either. Since you wisely demand the space to go through your own process, please be nice to others while they go through their processes, too.

Another suggestion that I suggest taking earnestly is that you look at your behaviors and notice what you do to keep your emotions suppressed. Do you smoke? Do you use drugs or alcohol? How about caffeine? Do you use sex to suppress your feelings? Food, maybe? How about television? Acknowledge the truth about your suppressive habits. Suppression creates the illusion that it makes you feel better; what it really does is keep your emotions from getting processed, robs you of energy, wastes your time and your life, and keeps you stuck. Stop doing whatever you habitually do to suppress your emotions.

If you have difficulty stopping, consider these three suggestions: 1. Vivation is extremely helpful in breaking any kind of bad habit because it enables you to make peace with the feelings that come up as you quit. 2. You may want to consider finding a good psychotherapist. A good therapist may be able to help you work out why you are having such a need to use the suppressive mechanism. 3. Consider joining one of the many excellent "Twelve Step" programs, that are based on the formula of Alcoholics Anonymous. These programs exist for almost every bad habit imaginable, nowadays. They work extremely well and give you a supportive community that you might never get to experience in any other way. You certainly have nothing to lose by going to a meeting or two.

It is extremely helpful to have a supportive community somehow. If you don't have a sense of that and you don't see a supportive community that you want to join, take the initiative to start one. Simply contact everyone you can think of that you would like to have as a part of your community of support and plan activities together. The more shared experiences your group has the more cohesive your community will be. If you have a shared, clear purpose for your group, all the better.

At various stages of your Creativity Program you may find certain psychological blocks to creativity coming up. Here are a few common ones with some simple solutions.

If you find yourself having problems with fear — fear of success, fear of failure, or really any kind of fear — try these two ideas: 1. Learn to enjoy the feeling of fear. Vivation can greatly assist you in this. Try doing Vivation while riding roller coasters or skydiving. Put yourself in situations where you'll have to do public speaking and Vive into the feelings you have about that. If you get to where you don't mind the feeling of fear, it won't cause you any trouble at all. 2. Just do what is on-purpose for achieving your goal whether or not your feel afraid. Just do it anyway. If you do that a few times, fear will lose its grip on you.

You may find parental conditioning getting in your way. Maybe you're afraid your parents will disapprove of you if you do things you really want to. One suggestion I have for this is that if you have this problem and you are depending on your parents for anything, financial assistance or anything else, do anything it takes to become independent, find any other way to live without depending on them.

Another suggestion for a creative way to handle problems with parental conditioning is that, if you work in any art form, try portraying in your art form your relationship with your parents. For example, if you are a musician, singer, composer, etc., write and even perform a composition that captures for you the tone of your relationship with your parents. If you paint, paint a picture of it. If you write, write about it. This works tremendously well. You can also write letters to your parents expressing your exact thoughts and feelings and then either mail them or not.

Perfectionism is a real enemy of creativity for many people. It can get in the way in more than one way. Sometimes perfectionists never do much at all because they are so afraid it won't be good enough. Other times perfectionists take far too long to complete a project. Learn to appreciate imperfection. Learn to like the way imperfection makes something unique. Really seek out the beauty in imperfection of every kind. Give everything the chance to be perfect in its own way rather than having to be perfect in your way. Work with the affirmation "I love everything that's below my standards" until you get it.

Yet another common block to creativity is one that I call "Waiting for the Muse." Many people think they should feel inspired first and then do something. I'll tell you, that's the hard way to do it. If you're a writer, I suggest writing as much as you can, whether you feel inspired or not. Write anything, letters, erotica, anything is better than nothing. Do lots of Discovery Writing. Similarly, if you sculpt, sculpt a lot. If you compose, compose a lot. Don't wait for anything.

Most of the time you will find that your inspiration comes from your projects, not the other way around.

If you have done the processes in this book, then you have a much clearer sense of yourself than when you started. You know what you want, you know what makes your heart sing. You know how to have access to your creativity reliably and how to use that for accomplisging the things that are most important to you. Now get on with it, do it now, go for it!

There are no limits to what you can do now that your creativity is engaged. Dare to think grandly. Dare to have your fondest dream fulfilled!

ABOUT THE AUTHOR

I was born in San Bernardino, California, in 1955. I lived there until I moved to the neighboring town, Riverside, where I attended the University of California. I had a dual major of Religious Studies and Computer Science. I am not now religious and I'm no hacker, either. I wouldn't dream of writing without my computer, though.

My late father, Al Leonard, was a skilled civilian maintenance mechanic working for the Air Force, fixing virtually any kind of machinery except aircraft. My mother, Anna Lee Leonard, was for many years a top saleswoman; she's retired now. I have three older sisters, Alona Forsberg, Linda Nathan and Susan Wolfe. Susan is a successful author, too, of mystery novels.

In 1979, I developed the modern process of Vivation. Several influences were important to my creation of this process, including kundalini yoga, rebirthing, and most important, a remarkable experience I had while climbing a mountain one morning in 1972. That experience gave me the insights that led to the whole concept of emotional integration and really the entire underlying philosophy of the Vivation process. Vivation is not a synthesis of other processes and influences — it came about as a result of my own observation and insight into how people experience and process their feelings.

In 1982, my friend Phil Laut and I wrote the first book on Vivation, *Vivation — The Science of Enjoying All of Your Life*. That book has been successfully published by Phil's Company, Vivation Publishing Company, since 1983, and is available now in German, French, Italian and Dutch, as well as English. Since May of 1985, I have been teaching seminars all over the world on approximately 35 weekends per year. I intend to continue leading seminars on approximately that schedule for all the foreseeable future.

I started work on this book in December, 1986. I have finished it now on the last day of April, 1989.

I'm an attractive guy with a great sense of humor and a successful career. I am unmarried and highly eligible.

At this writing I lead two different weekend seminars for the public:

The Vivation in Action Weekend is a complete seminar on mastering the Vivation process for autonomous use. I can teach you how to master Vivation for yourself in a single weekend. I have led this seminar, at this writing, over 120 times, for thousands of participants, throughout the United States, Canada and Europe.

The Power of Creativity Weekend also has Vivation in it, and otherwise consists of a whole series of processes to help you eliminate your blocks to creativity, discover what would fulfill you the most, and apply your creativity well to that. This seminar is very much fun and very practical, too.

I also lead Vivation Professional Trainings two or three times a year. These are seventeen days long and are complete training to have a career as a Vivation Professional, which is without a doubt the most enjoyable and fulfilling career imaginable.

For businesses I lead two special creativity seminars: The Power of Creativity for Management Professionals and The Power of Creativity for Salespeople.

My seminar leadership style is characterized by thoroughness, sensitivity to the needs of the participants, humor, practicality and of course creativity.

If you would like to be informed of my seminar schedule, just phone or write.

Additionally, you might be interested in hosting a seminar for me in your city. This can be a highly lucrative business venture for you. My seminars are usually booked about six months to one year ahead. Please phone or write about that, too.

I also enjoy going on TV and radio shows as often as I can. What I like to talk about on shows is ways that members of the audience can tap into their creativity immediately and put it to practical use in their lives. If you are connected with a show, please contact me.

I am very open to participating in well thought-out scientific research on Vivation and/or creativity. Feel very free to contact me about that, too.

Phone or write:
JIM LEONARD
INTERNATIONAL VIVATION COMMUNITY
PO Box 567713
Atlanta, GA 30356
(404) 551-8626.

ABOUT THE COVER ARTIST

Robert Ray Baker has been working with visionary art since 1978. In 1984, he recognized his life's dream and began using air brush painting as the focus of his artistic expression. Robert approaches his craft through meditation, dream work, prayer, ceremony and magic, reaching into himself and bringing forth visual beauty through the use of ancient symbols and pure colors alive with the human spirit. He is a self-taught artist using over twenty years of personal inner work as his resource, painting what he finds and experiences within and around the universe. His painted works ask unanswerable questions, challenge the social norms, re-awaken the ancient ways and are helping bring new concepts into existence.

He may be reached at his studio at 611 N. Locust St., Denton, TX 76201 Phone: 817-382-0732

ABOUT THE ILLUSTRATOR

The pencil illustrations at the start of each chapter and part are the work of Atlanta artist, Lloyd Nick.

Lloyd Nick was born in Rochester, New York. He received his liberal arts and fine arts training at Hunter College of the City University of New York (BFA) and the University of Pennsylvania (MFA). He was the recipient of special national awards which enabled him to expand his studies in painting at Yale Norfolk Summer School and the Skowhegan School of Painting and Sculpture.

During the 1970's he received a National Endowment of the Humanities grant to research the creative aspects of Claude Monet's landscape painting in Giverny, France; during the same period he painted and exhibited regularly in Europe and represented the United States in a three-week international painting seminar in northern Yugoslavia and had exhibitions in Monaco, Yugoslavia and Bulgaria.

His academic experience includes college teaching often chairing art departments in Philadelphia; Monte Carlo, Monaco; Rochester, New York; Greensboro and Fayetteville, North Carolina. Presently he is serving as Director of Art Programs which includes the directorship of the art museum at Oglethorpe University in Atlanta, Georgia.

Other related professional appointments have been as art critic for Gannett Newspapers, member of the Board of Trustees of the Nicholas Roerich Museum in New York City and membership of state and local arts councils.

He has a broad exhibition and collectors record. His works are present international collections which include those of Princess Grace of Monaco, British pianist Moura Lympany, AT&T, Barclays Bank, Burlington Industries, Duke University Hospital and others.

Lloyd Nick's mediums are painting, drawing and stone lithography and over a twenty year period has developed a horizontal landscape format including eastern and western historical and philosophical concepts and proportions like the golden section, for example. His humanistic approach towards art results in the belief that the intuitive or the spiritual must be present in art; in fact, it is visceral in the visual image.

CARTOON CREDITS

SUGGESTED READING

ON HAVING CREATIVE BREAKTHROUGHS:
Vivation the Science of Enjoying All of Your Life, by Jim Leonard and Phil Laut (Vivation Publishing Co., Cincinnati, Ohio)
A Whack on the Side of the Head, by Roger Oech (Warner, New York)
Conceptual Blockbusting, by James L. Adams (Addison-Wesley Co., Reading, Mass.)

CREATIVE APPROACHES TO CAREER AND PROSPERITY:
Money Is My Friend, by Phil Laut (Vivation Publishing Co., Cincinnati, Ohio)
Moneylove, by Jerry Gillies (Warner, New York)
How to Master the Art of Sales, by Tom Hopkins (Warner, New York)

CREATIVE APPROACHES TO INTIMATE RELATIONSHIPS
Love, Sex, and Communication for Everyone by Jeanne Miller and Phil Laut (Vivation Publishing Co., Cincinnati, Ohio)
I Deserve Love, by Sondra Ray (Celestial Arts, Berkeley, Calif.)

CREATIVE APPROACHES TO HEALTH:
The Only Diet There Is, by Sondra Ray (Celestial Arts, Berkeley, Calif.)
Energy Medicine, by Laurence Badgley, M.D. (Human Energy Press, San Bruno, Calif.)

MATERIALS APPENDIX

Here's how to get the cards made for the Values Process, the Creative Time Management process, etc.:

1. Call up your nearest printer or photocopy store and ask if they have a cutting machine. If they do, go there. If not, keep calling until you find the nearest one that does. Almost all printers have them and many photocopy stores do.

2. For "blank business cards" tell them to cut white card stock to business card size, i.e., 2"x3½". A thousand of these should cost less than $15.00.

3. For the "category cards" in the time management system choose some card stock of a color you like and have them cut you about 50 of these, ¼" longer than business card size, i.e., 2"x3¾". These should cost about the same per card as the white ones, perhaps very slightly more.

4. This entire job will only take someone maybe 10 minutes at most.

Creative Source in El Toro, California, also makes available the following supplies, related to this book:

MATERIALS LIST

Detail Schedule Pages	
Pack of 200	12.95
Detail Schedule 200 pages with	
three ring Binder and calendar	25.00
How to Use Discovery Writing to Achieve	
any Goal (11 page description andpre-printed blanks for	
process in Chapter 3)	15.00
Time management Cards	
500 blank white card and 50 colored category cards	25.00

Wholesale inquiries welcome.

The Creative Source
PO Box 11024
Costa Mesa, CA 92627 USA
Phone: 714-458-7971

A Worldwide Listing of Vivation™ Professionals

ALASKA
Sheri Miller, AVP
1828 Kennedy St.
Fairbanks, AK 99709
(907) 474-0662

ARKANSAS
Herb Pablo, AVP
PO Box 2751
West Memphis, AR 72301
(501) 732-1238
(501) 732-1154

CALIFORNIA (Southern)
Eve Jones, AVP
140 S. Norton Ave.
Los Angeles, CA 90004
(213) 839-4378

Lee Kuntz, AVP
3627 Keystone Ave. #2
Los Angeles, CA 90034
(213) 839-4378

Patricia Bacall, AVP
400 S. Beverly Dr. #214
Beverly Hills, CA 90212
213-937-7437

Sue & Flori Riggs, AVP
1041 Helix Ave.
Chula Vista, CA 92011
(619) 420-2161
(619) 426-6539

CALIFORNIA (Northern)
Anne Jill Leonard, AVP
2224 Seventeenth Ave.
San Francisco, CA 94116
(415) 753-0370

GEORGIA
Jim Leonard, AVP
PO Box 567713
Atlanta, GA 30356
(404) 551-8626

ILLINOIS
Pat Murrell, AVP
187 W. 19th
Alton, IL 62002
(618) 462-4051
(314) 569-5795

Steven Strauss, AVP
RR2 Box 173
Pleasant Plain, IL 62677
(214) 487-7104

MASSACHUSETTS
Sande Sharlat, AVP &
Tom Streit, AVP
218 Thorndike Place #104
Cambridge, MA 02141
(617) 494-6544

MARYLAND
Jonathan & Laura Bosch, AVP
805 Horton Dr.
Silver Spring, MD 20902
(301) 649-5813

MARYLAND (continued)
Susan R. Cox, AVP
414 4th Ave. Box 277
Washington Grove, MD 20880
(301) 258-0870 (Gaithersburg area)

Mary Kent Norton, AVP
398 Ridgely Ave.
Annapolis, MD 21401
(301) 268-2322

David Pierce, AVP
11602 Highview Ave.
Silver Spring, MD 20902
(301) 949-3686

MISSOURI
Pat Murrell, AVP
PO Box 23305
St. Louis, MO 63156
(618) 462-4051
(314) 569-5795

NEVADA
Norma Viergutz, AVP
381 W. Berry Creek Ct.
Elko, NV 89801
(702) 738-7574

NORTH CAROLINA
Michael McDowell, AVP
1014 Burch Ave.
Durham, NC 27701
(919) 493-9354

Charles Smith, AVP
2117 St. Mary St.
Raleigh, NC 27608
(919) 781-7636
(919) 781-4743

OHIO
Phil Laut, AVP
Jeanne Miller, AVP
PO Box 8269
Cincinnati, OH 45208
(513) 321-6411
(513) 321-4405

OREGON
Barbara Wayne, AVP
1804 NW Second St.
Bend, OR 97701
(503) 389-3977

PUERTO RICO
Raul G. Gaya, Jr., AVP
103 Mallorca
Floral Park, PR 00919
(809) 728-7276
(809) 726-3032

TEXAS
Joan Bolmer, AVP
One Woodbranch Center
11931 Wickchester #200
Houston, TX 77043
(713) 530-9687

Harlin Magee, AVP
New Creation Seminars
PO Box 181111
Austin, TX 78718
(512) 339-1305

Peggy Pratt, AVP
PO Box 13492
Arlington, TX 76094
(817) 792-3218

VIRGINIA
Jim & Bev Worsley, AVP
Rt. 1 Box 12-A
Afton, VA 22920
(703) 456-8655

CANADA
Judy Gane, AVP
Vivation Institute of Canada
54 Tivoli Drive
Hamilton, ONT L9C 2E4
(416) 389-8737

Amanda Vaughan, AVP
3588 W. 18th Ave.
Vancouver, BC V6S 1B1
(604) 736-4665

ASSOCIATED VIVATION PROFESSIONALS
PO Box 8269
Cincinnati, OH 45208 USA

A referral service for Vivation Professionals. You can receive a list of Vivation Professionals in your area and additional information about Vivation by phoning: (800) 829-2625 in the United States or Canada or (513) 321-4405.

Vivation is a service mark and publishing trademark of Jim Leonard, Anne Jill Leonard, Phil Laut and Jeanne Miller, doing business as Associated Vivation Professionals.

Some of the members of Associated Vivation Professionals are listed above. They are indicated with AVP next to their names.

The following people, although not Vivation Professionals, are professional rebirthers who use methods similar to Vivation:

CALIFORNIA (Northern)
Lois Hochenauer
1452 Cortez Ct.
Walnut Creek, CA 94598
(415) 939-3863

Bob Frissell
5155 Simoni Ct.
El Sobrante, CA 94803
(415) 222-4059

COLORADO
Ken Rosevear
5061 S. Zinnia Ct.
Morrison, CO 80465
(303) 973-9859

CONNECTICUT
Nikki Gazda
36 Horizon Hill
Newington, CT 06111
203-667-2689

MASSACHUSETTS
Joanne Kelly
PO Box 583
Stockbridge, MA 01262
(413) 243-1767

NEW HAMPSHIRE
Earthstar/Dovestar
50 Whitehall Rd.
Hooksett, NH 03016
(603) 669-9497

NEW YORK
Rosetta DeGillio
525 E. 88th St. #1B
New York, NY 10128
(212) 734-9060

Charlotte Friedman
57 W. 75th St. #7E
New York, NY 10023
(212) 362-0015

Denise Gilman
59 Eastchester Rd.
New Rochelle, NY 10801
(914) 636-1979

TENNESSEE
Betty Hutto
147 Jefferson Ave. #1000
Memphis, TN 38103
(901) 525-7001
(901) 728-6288

VIRGINIA
Ken Kizer & Renee Seise
10613 Patterson Ave.
Richmond, VA 23233
(804) 740-9239

Ravi Ray Torbert
PO Box 166
Virginia Beach, VA 23458
(804) 481-2923

ENGLAND
Hilary Newman
79-A Acre Lane
London, SW2 5TN
U.K.
(01) 733-9774

ORDER FORM

Vivation Publishing Co.
P.O. Box 8269
Cincinnati, Ohio 45208
USA

In a hurry?
We accept orders on VISA
and Mastercard.
Phone (513) 321-4405

Name (Please print clearly)
_____

Address
_____

City/State/Zip

Total Amount of Order _____

For Credit card payments
_____

Card Number
_____

Expiration Date
_____

Signature

BOOKS	Quantity	Amount	TAPES	Quantity	Amount
$9.95 Money Is My Friend New, expanded edition	_____	_____	$20.00 Money Is an Intentional Creation of the Mind (two tape set)	_____	_____
$9.95 Rebirthing: The Science of Enjoying All of Your Life	_____	_____	$20.00 Principles of Personal Financial Success (two tape set)	_____	_____
$15.95 Your Fondest Dream	_____	_____	$10.00 Reclaiming Your Personal Power	_____	_____
$12.95 Love, Sex and Communication for Everyone Pub. Date 12/01/89	_____	_____			

SUB TOTAL

(Ohio residents, please add 5.5% sales tax) _____

Shipping (please add $1.00 per item,
shipping free on orders more than $35.00) _____

GRAND TOTAL _____

☐ Check here if you wish to receive wholesale ordering information.
☐ Please send me a coupon for 25% savings on your Money Is My Friend Weekend Seminar
☐ Please send me a coupon for 25% savings on your Love, Sex and Communication Weekend Seminar
☐ I want to become a Vivation Professional. Please phone me about Professional Trainings.
☐ Please send me information about the Vivation Professionals in my area.

Y1

ORDER FORM

Vivation Publishing Co.
P.O. Box 8269
Cincinnati, Ohio 45208
USA

In a hurry?
We accept orders on VISA
and Mastercard.
Phone (513) 321-4405

Name (Please print clearly)
_____

Address
_____

City/State/Zip

Total Amount of Order _____

For Credit card payments
_____

Card Number
_____

Expiration Date
_____

Signature

BOOKS	Quantity	Amount	TAPES	Quantity	Amount
$9.95 Money Is My Friend New, expanded edition	_____	_____	$20.00 Money Is an Intentional Creation of the Mind (two tape set)	_____	_____
$9.95 Rebirthing: The Science of Enjoying All of Your Life	_____	_____	$20.00 Principles of Personal Financial Success (two tape set)	_____	_____
$15.95 Your Fondest Dream	_____	_____	$10.00 Reclaiming Your Personal Power	_____	_____
$12.95 Love, Sex and Communication for Everyone Pub. Date 12/01/89	_____	_____			

SUB TOTAL

(Ohio residents, please add 5.5% sales tax) _____

Shipping (please add $1.00 per item,
shipping free on orders more than $35.00) _____

GRAND TOTAL _____

☐ Check here if you wish to receive wholesale ordering information.
☐ Please send me a coupon for 25% savings on your Money Is My Friend Weekend Seminar
☐ Please send me a coupon for 25% savings on your Love, Sex and Communication Weekend Seminar
☐ I want to become a Vivation Professional. Please phone me about Professional Trainings.
☐ Please send me information about the Vivation Professionals in my area.

Y1

BUSINESS REPLY MAIL

FIRST CLASS   PERMIT NO. 17278   CINCINNATI, OH

POSTAGE WILL BE PAID BY ADDRESSEE

Vivation Publishing Co.
P.O. Box 8269
Cincinnati, Ohio 45208
U.S.A.

BUSINESS REPLY MAIL

FIRST CLASS   PERMIT NO. 17278   CINCINNATI, OH

POSTAGE WILL BE PAID BY ADDRESSEE

Vivation Publishing Co.
P.O. Box 8269
Cincinnati, Ohio 45208
U.S.A.